May you joyfully
prepare for the day
When He Shall Appear

Bonnie B. Robinson

When He Shall Appear

Bonnie B. Robinson

Bonfire Press, LC
Salt Lake City, UT

Bonfire Press, LC
171 East Third Avenue, #708
Salt Lake City, UT 84103
www.bonfirepress.com

Copyright © 2006 Bonnie B. Robinson
First printing, July 2006
Printed in the United States of America

Cover art: "The Resurrected Jesus Christ" by Grant Romney Clawson
© by Intellectual Reserve, Inc.
Used by permission

Cover design: © 2006 Bonfire Press, LC
Photograph of the author is courtesy of Eric Bjorklund, Acclaim Photography

ISBN–13: 978-1-931858-07-6
ISBN–10: 1-931858-07-6

To Glenn,
for time and all eternity.

We know that, when he shall appear
we shall be like him; for we shall see him as he is.
And every man that hath this hope in him
purifieth himself, even as he is pure.
1 John 3:2-3

Acknowledgements

This book might never have come forth without the influence of Karlene Browning at Rosehaven Publishing and Distribution, or Jay Van Dyke at Whitehall Printing Company.

A huge *thank you* goes to my friends who read the manuscript and provided support and encouragement: Barbara Smith, Sherry Meidell, Kathleen Anderson, and especially Christine Graham for her skilled editing.

I love and appreciate my family, especially my husband Glenn Robinson, who understood my need to devote time to this endeavor.

I am grateful for ancient prophets, called of God to compose scriptures that draw us near to Him. Thank you to modern-day prophets, apostles, and other leaders of The Church of Jesus Christ of Latter-day Saints for sharing edifying words of God—many of their thoughts inspired the writing of this book.

Foremost, I express my gratitude to God the Eternal Father who gave my spirit life and to Jesus Christ who offers rebirth into eternal realms.

Contents

chapters

Prologue

One Sunday morning before my alarm sounded, I had a disquieting dream. I saw myself drive to church, park my car, then enter the building amid a feverish bustle of people. I knew the excitement wasn't because I'd arrived five minutes early rather than five minutes late. Nor was it that they'd noticed my new dress rather than the old one I'd worn three weeks in a row. Everyone in the corridors seemed truly agitated, unsettled. Some had gathered to chat in tense whispers. Others stood thoughtfully alone or paced the floor, as if wondering whether to stay at church or return home. Their countenances varied from exhilaration to dismay.

While I scrutinized the strange scene, a friend rushed up to exclaim, "Jesus is coming to church! Jesus is coming to church!"

My throat tightened as I questioned the inconceivable: "Jesus is coming to church?"

"I've got to check my lipstick," my friend said as she turned toward the restroom.

Lipstick? I thought. *Why is that important? Jesus is coming to church!* Still stunned, I endeavored simply to breathe. Inhale. Exhale. *Jesus is coming to church!*

As if hit by a stun gun, I could do nothing but stand idly amid the fuss and flurry. I saw two teenaged brothers roughly elbow each other, as though no adjustment was needed in their rowdy behavior, despite the soon-to-be Advent. I smelled vague odors of ammonia and furniture wax, used by people tidying the meetinghouse. Two women polished the glass double doors, another one shined the drinking fountain, and a ward clerk neatly arranged lost-and-found articles above the coat rack.

I had previously experienced the combined thrill and anxiety of a prophet of God arriving for a meeting. But a visitation by Christ? Sheer joy trumpeted through me! Yet simultaneously, I felt my lack of preparation and sensed other deficiencies within myself. Like most Latter-day Saints, I had attempted to live a good life. Oh, I may have fudged once or twice on the truth about completing my visiting teaching. And there was that time I complained about Sunday taking up one-seventh of my life. But I'd never resorted to using foul language like "flip" or "fetch."

While I sleuthed through a mental list of my weaknesses, I observed that some of my fellow Saints showed concern only for their physical deportment. Several men straightened their ties and shirt collars, while women smoothed wrinkles from their dresses or realigned loose strands of hair.

Despite the fidgety adults and teens, the young children in the foyer seemed unusually docile, except for a three-year-old who tugged on his father's pant leg. After a whisper from his older sister, the boy quieted, sat down on the plum-colored carpet, and rested his chin in his hands as if in deep contemplation. I recalled Christ's admonition that we become like children, or at least personify childlike qualities, to be received in the kingdom of God. It's easy to see why. Not only are children cuter, but, like puppies, kittens, and lambs, they are softer and more loveable than fully-grown animals. Humans might be better off dying before the accountable baptismal age of eight, rather than struggling to remain soft-hearted in this sin-filled world.

A sudden roaring vacuum jarred me from my reverie. The intrusive machine veered at my feet and trailed dust across my black shoes. Though I could have stooped to give them a quick spit-shine, I knew the Savior would not care as much about my outward appearance as He did about the depths of my soul.

That thought sent me spiraling through deeper introspection. Wasn't I a good mother, allowing our front yard to be landscaped by bikes undergoing repairs and leftover snack boxes that had rotted in rainfall? I'd only missed one canning assignment in the last year, and I never displayed my temple recommend as a check protection card. Why didn't I feel spiritually prepared to meet the Lord? How should I behave in His presence? Did I, or anyone else, fully comprehend the significance of this miraculous unveiling?

I laid a hand against the cool brick wall to steady myself. Would a choir be singing, like the heavenly hosts who proclaimed the Lord's birth? I wondered if I might be asked to join them, though I could never get through an audition for the Mormon Tabernacle Choir. I was counting on the sudden need for a multitude of voices, since it's prophesied that the righteous will join angels to herald Christ's Second Coming. Yet how did today's Sabbath appearance mesh with those prophecies?

As the hallways filled with more families, the earnest phrase echoed: "Jesus is coming to church! Jesus is coming to church!"

Overcome by both elation and self-doubt, my knees weakened, and I knew I must sit down. With measured steps, I crossed the crowded foyer and stopped at the chapel doors to peer inside. Awe and reverence permeated the room with tangible peace. A few dozen adults and children sat scattered among the familiar wooden benches. Some read their scriptures, while others had their heads bowed in prayer or meditation. I was intrigued by the soft light that seemed to radiate from their countenances. Rather than the usual organ prelude, a child faintly sang, "Lead me, guide me, walk beside me, Help me find the way." Near the doorway, an older man worshipfully admired a portrait of Christ in a lesson manual. Tears trickled over the rims of his aged eyelids.

What a contrast between the people in the corridors, concerned with mere temporal tasks, and those in the chapel who had groomed themselves spiritually for the Lord's arrival! I could only wonder where I belonged. What was it that John said? "And *now*, little children, abide in him; that, *when he shall appear*, we may have confidence, and not be ashamed before him at his coming" (1 John 2:28, italics added). Was it too late for me to change *now?* This wasn't a case when I could take two doses of humility and call God in the morning. Either I was ready for the Lord's arrival or I was not.

How I yearned to separate myself from the harried foyer behind me. Yet if I tiptoed forward, would guilt tiptoe through me? Was my spirit truly contrite, my heart broken, and my soul overflowing with love for my Redeemer, Jesus Christ?

As I stood on this threshold of decision, the alarm on my bedside table awakened me from the dream. With a reluctant sigh, I shoved aside my cozy covers and readied myself for the Sabbath. Yet I could not shove aside the lingering questions: Should I be paying more attention to the signs of the Last Days, since we "know neither the day nor the hour wherein the Son of man cometh"? (Matthew 25:13). Though He "shall send his angels with a great sound of a trumpet" (Matthew 24:31), will my ears be divinely attuned to hear the announcement? Will my spiritual eyesight be acute enough to see Him appear in clouds of glory? How can I better prepare for the day when He appears? Am I infused with a desire to become like Him? Do I thoroughly know Him so I will recognize Him when he comes?

President Howard W. Hunter said, "We must know Christ better than we know him; we must remember him more often than we remember him; we must serve him more valiantly than we serve him." ("What Manner of Men Ought Ye to Be?" *Ensign*, May 1994, 64)

This book will explore several soul-stretching ideas. I invite you to travel its pages and find the passageway to prepare for the Second Coming of Jesus Christ.

"[For] we know that, when he shall appear we shall be like him; for we shall see him as he is.

"And every man that hath this hope in him purifieth himself, even as he is pure" (1 John 3:2–3).

And this is life eternal,
that they might know thee the only true God,
and Jesus Christ, whom thou has sent.
John 17:3

Know God and Jesus Christ

Every gospel discussion should start with a reminder of God's declaration of intent: "For behold, this is my work and my glory—to bring to pass the immortality and eternal life of man" (Moses 1:39). So are you ready for this in-depth journey? Make sure your chair is upright and your seatbelt snapped in place. Please remove any cumbersome jewelry, especially nose rings or tongue piercings, then keep your arms and legs inside this heavenward trip at all times. If you should feel faint of heart and require assistance, do not expect an oxygen mask to automatically drop from overhead. It's up to you to contact your Father in Heaven directly through prayer. That said, we may proceed.

To acquire immortality and eternal life means to live in the same manner as Heavenly Father and Jesus Christ. Although mortal men and women may not fully comprehend the majesty of a celestial lifestyle, that should not impede anyone from seeking such glory.

During His intercessory prayer, Jesus said, "And this is life eternal, that they might know thee the only true God, and Jesus Christ, whom thou has sent" (John 17:30). Therefore, the main reason to gain knowledge of the Father and Son is to attain eternal life. Gain to attain. Sounds easy enough. We aren't required to know the unknowable, such as the location of the ancient City of Enoch. We don't have to memorize all the important verses in the Bible and Book of Mormon and therefore win every scripture chase competition. We are asked only to know "the only true God, and Jesus Christ." However, this means far more than to intellectually know *about* Them—for example, learning how our Father created His children, or reading stories of Jesus healing people. To know Them is to exercise unending faith in Their power and love. To know Them is to allow Their divine influence to penetrate our daily thoughts and behavior.

One day while driving downtown, I passed a sign for a restaurant. The "s" was gone, so it read "re taurant." Did the absent letter mean something was also missing in the quality of the restaurant—that the food or service was substandard? Likewise, is there something missing in the quality of our lives if we only know *about* Heavenly Father and Jesus Christ and don't fully comprehend Their profound attributes of character? Becoming like the Father and Son implies that we know Them well enough to replicate, duplicate, and emulate Their sacred traits within ourselves.

From time to time we may get glimpses of our own divine inheritance—those marvelous, miraculous stretches of the soul—when we experience Their supreme power and love as motivators in our lives. Then we can truly *know* God and reflect His image in our countenance (see Alma 5:14). Our eternal potential as sons and daughters of God is limitless, even on days when we seem to be trapped in our humanness. Remember that Christ also spent many years as a mortal being. He understands the vicissitudes and uncertainties of life on earth. It's vital for us to learn from His example, overcome the cares of the world, and develop sublime qualities of character.

As the Son of God, Jesus Christ is now a resurrected being, and He is in every aspect the same as our Heavenly Father. To learn of one is to learn of the other, as Elder Bruce R. McConkie wrote:

"In the exalted family of the Gods, the Father and the Son are one. They have the same character, perfections, and attributes. They think the same thoughts, speak the same words, perform the same acts, have the same desires, and do the same works. They possess the same power, have the same mind, know the same truths, live in the same light and glory. To know one is to know the other; to see one is to see the other; to hear the voice of one is to hear the voice of the other. Their unity is perfect. [*The Promised Messiah*, 9]

During seasons of my life, when piles of kids' grimy clothes and sinks full of dirty dishes demanded immediate attention, I did not spend as much time as I should have studying the gospel. I fooled myself into believing I could wait until I was less exhausted to search and ponder the things of God. But I was wrong to delay my spiritual progress, because "Whatever principle of intelligence we attain unto in this life, it will rise with us in the resurrection.

"And if a person gains more knowledge and intelligence in this life through his diligence and obedience than another, he will have so much the advantage in the world to come" (D&C 130:18-19).

Did you catch those words again? *Attain* and *gain.* As our desire for knowledge expands, it may seem the gap of our lackings grows wider. It's that principle of "the more I know, the more I realize I don't know."

Heavenly Father and Jesus Christ are merciful and kind, and They continue to occupy Their days with the business of saving our souls. I'm edified by President Gordon B. Hinckley's words, "Miracle of miracles and wonder of wonders, they are interested in us, and we are the substance of their great concern. They are available to each of us. We approach the Father through the Son. He is our intercessor at the throne of God. How marvelous it is that we may so speak to the Father in the name of the Son." ("The Father, Son, and Holy Ghost," *Ensign*, Nov. 1986, 51)

Unlike many religions in the world, The Church of Jesus Christ of Latter-day Saints clearly delineates the channel by which we approach God the Father: we go through Jesus Christ. This

restored gospel provides many reasons to acquire knowledge of
the Father and Son while we live on earth.

The First Principle of the Gospel

In the thirteen Articles of Faith, written by divine inspiration,
Joseph Smith placed the foremost as Article One: "We believe in
God, the Eternal Father, and in His Son, Jesus Christ, and in the
Holy Ghost." In addition, Joseph Smith declared from the pulpit,
"It is the first principle of the gospel to know for a certainty the
character of God" (*History of the Church*, 6:305).

The foundation of this gospel is belief in the Godhead. Each
person on earth falls somewhere in the spectrum from non-belief
to simple belief, then to faith, then knowledge, and lastly, total
comprehension of all spiritual matters. Joseph Smith emphasized
why it is vital to increase our knowledge of God.

> Having a knowledge of God, we begin to know how to approach
> Him, and how to ask so as to receive an answer.
> When we understand the character of God, and know how to
> come to Him, he begins to unfold the heavens to us, and to tell
> us all about it. When we are ready to come to him, he is ready
> to come to us....
> The relationship we have with God places us in a situation
> to advance in knowledge. He has power to institute laws to
> instruct the weaker intelligences, that they may be exalted
> with Himself, so that they might have one glory upon another,
> and all that knowledge, power, glory, and intelligence, which is
> requisite in order to save them in the world of spirits. [*History
> of the Church*, 6:308, 312]

What a blessing that God wants us to progress like Himself
toward greater intelligence, power, and glory! How remarkable for
mere mortals to advance toward magnificence like our Heavenly
Father's! Maybe then I will finally learn to balance my checkbook.
Though it may take all eternity to achieve godliness, it's humbling
to know we were created for that very purpose.

God Is Our Creator

Many scriptures denote God the Father as the original creator and organizer of the heavens above and the earth on which we live. "The scriptures are laid before thee, yea, and all things denote there is a God; yea, even the earth, and all things that are upon the face of it, yea, and its motion, yea, and also all the planets which move in their regular form do witness that there is a Supreme Creator" (Alma 30:44).

The scriptures don't describe a "big bang theory" or relate other scientific conjectures on the creation of the universe. We only know that God spoke and the elements obeyed. God the Father acted as the supreme architect and designer, while Jesus Christ became the chief contractor performing the work. "And worlds without number have I created; and I also created them for mine own purpose; and by the Son I created them, which is mine Only Begotten" (Moses 1:33-34).

It's important to delineate the difference between the words *create* and *organize,* since Joseph Smith was precise about those terms: "Now, the word create came from the word *baurau,* which does not mean to create out of nothing; it means to organize; the same as a man would organize materials and build a ship. Hence we infer that God had materials to organize the world out of chaos—chaotic matter, which is element" (*History of the Church,* 6:308, italics in the original).

God also created the inhabitants upon the earth, "male and female, after his own image and in his own likeness, created he them" (D&C 20:18). That seems a logical reason for wanting to know God. Of course, humans are not always known for logic. I've seen more than one "wet paint" sign, where people go and touch the wall then wonder why they get paint on their fingers.

God Comprehends All Things

A quest for increased intelligence should begin with a recognition that we can learn more from God than from any other source. "He comprehendeth all things, and all things are before him, and all things are round about him; and he is above all things, and in all things, and is through all things, and is round about all things; and all things are by him, and of him, even God, forever and ever" (D&C 88:41).

Although the word *omniscient* does not appear in the scriptures, it is an apt description for the infinite and all-knowing power of God. Ammon rejoiced in God's omniscience: "My joy is carried away, even unto boasting in my God; for he has all power, all wisdom, and all understanding; he comprehendeth all things" (Alma 26:35).

We, too, should extol the infinite knowledge which the Father and Son possess. Jesus is "the true light that lighteth every man that cometh into the world" (D&C 93:2). A portion of His light dwells within us. When He enlightens our spirits, our knowledge of truth increases. "And the light which shineth, which giveth you light, is through him who enlighteneth your eyes, which is the same light that quickeneth your understanding" (D&C 88:11).

Intelligence Subdues Darkness

Knowledge of truth can protect us from Satan's evil designs. "The glory of God is intelligence, or, in other words, light and truth. Light and truth forsake that evil one" (D&C 93:36-37).

Intelligence, light, and truth are synonymous. Because they provide spiritual insight for the children of God, they can also subdue darkness and evil. I'm grateful Heavenly Father separated light from darkness before the foundation of this world.

And the earth was without form, and void; and I caused darkness to come upon the face of the deep;...
And I, God, said: Let there be light; and there was light.
And I, God, saw the light; and that light was good. And I, God, divided the light from the darkness" (Moses 2:2-4).

When God "caused darkness to come upon the face of the deep," does that mean He brought it from hiding as an anomaly in the universe? Often darkness is concealed, secretive, and difficult to discern. Perhaps that is why God made light to appear distinct and disunited from darkness. Then, as with all His creations, He called the light "good."

I am reminded of the schoolboy, who, while studying the inventions of Thomas Edison, said to his teacher, "When Edison made light, he stole God's idea."

In the creation scriptures God began by bringing forth light and dividing it from darkness. Yet it's not until later verses that He specifically fashioned the sun, moon, and stars (see Genesis 1:1-4,14-17; Moses 2:1-4, 14-18; Abraham 4:1-4,14-18). It used to confuse me how God could divide light from darkness before creating those specific orbs. Then I more closely examined a few verses in the Pearl of Great Price.

> And the earth, after it was formed, was empty and desolate, because they had not formed anything but the earth; and darkness reigned upon the face of the deep,...
>
> And they (the Gods) said: Let there be light; and there was light.
>
> And they (the Gods) comprehended the light, for it was bright; and they divided the light, or caused it to be divided, from the darkness. [Abraham 4:2-4]

When the Gods comprehended the light, I believe that meant more than the difference between daylight and nighttime. Intelligent people are often described as "bright." Perhaps the initial bright light the Gods comprehended was truth, which had to be isolated from the opposing darkness, or that which was void of truth.

As an outdoor enthusiast, I enjoy observing nature while driving on scenic highways. At night it can be difficult to see, particularly in wooded areas, where deer or other wildlife might suddenly appear on the highway. However, the driving I dislike most is near dusk or dawn, when the sun's rays slant sideways shadows of tree trunks onto the road. My eyes get stressed with alternating strokes of brightness then darkness across the windshield. Each ray of sun flashes a glare, so my pupils narrow to render me unable to readjust for the next dark phase.

The same blinding effect occurs when I hike sunny trails with slashes of shade from trees. The worst moment is with my first step into the shadow, where I might be surprised by tree roots, mud puddles, or jutting rocks that require quick side-stepping. Such experiences with mixed light and darkness have helped me understand why God caused light and truth to be totally divided from darkness and error.

Darkness is "symbolical of spiritual blindness or ignorance" and "of separation from God" (see "Darkness," Bible Dictionary). Jesus Christ and His gospel are incompatible with darkness and evil, for "in him was life; and the life was the light of men. And the light shineth in darkness; and the darkness comprehended it not" (John 1:4-5). Those who wish to be like Christ must radiate His absolute light, for "God is light, and in him is no darkness at all" (1 John 1:5).

Come Unto Me

During a family home evening, my husband, Glenn, tried to get a response from our four children. He said, "Remember the words Jesus spoke, 'Come _____?'" After no response, Glenn again prompted, "Come what?" There was a long pause, then our eight-year-old son said, "Come and get it?" For an energetic boy, always eager for a call to dinner, it was an apt response. Although the answer Glenn hoped for was "Come unto me" or "Come follow me," the phrase "Come and get it," was not too far off. Those who desire to "feast upon the words of Christ" (2 Nephi 32:3) can come and get every blessing God offers.

The scriptures are replete with Christ's invitations, saying "Come unto me," and "Come follow me." Yet many people attend to His beckoning blindly—not truly comprehending who it is they follow. Nor do they understand where He leads them, "because strait is the gate, and narrow is the way, which leadeth unto life, and few there be that find it" (Matthew 7:14).

I recall a prayer in church by a recently-returned sister missionary. In a humble tone, she said, "When the time comes, bless us that we might all get safely home." Though this can be a common phrase at church meetings, I sensed a deeper intent. Rather than "safely to our houses," the words suggested "safely home to our Heavenly Father."

Only one pair of nail-pierced feet mark the pathway we must follow, for Jesus is "the way, the truth, and the life: no man cometh unto the Father, but by [Him]" (John 14:6). Those who heed His voice and meekly walk with Him will reach eternal life.

Learn of Me

Perhaps the most basic reason to learn more of Jesus Christ is that He has invited us to do so: "Learn of me, and listen to my words; walk in the meekness of my Spirit, and you shall have peace in me" (D&C 19:23). The Lord's invitation to learn of Him is far more beneficial than any secular wisdom. Since I still have much spiritual knowledge to gain, I'll have to live forever. But I suppose that's the purpose of eternal life.

Once we undertake a dedicated study of God, we realize His all-inclusive invitation is meant to provide salvation for each one of His children. "Remember that there is no other way nor means whereby man can be saved, only through the atoning blood of Jesus Christ, who shall come; yea, remember that he cometh to redeem the world" (Helaman 5:9).

In every aspect of Christ's life—childhood, manhood, Godhood—He constantly showed who He was: the Beloved Son of God. Grasping the concept of His divine sonship may help us remember that we, too, are sons and daughters of Heavenly Father who loves us.

Understanding Ourselves

Those who seek added knowledge will receive it: "For behold, thus saith the Lord God: I will give unto the children of men line upon line, precept upon precept,... for they shall learn wisdom; for unto him that receiveth I will give more" (2 Nephi 28:30). Joseph

Smith taught that whatever we learn about the Father and Son will help us better comprehend ourselves.

> There are but a very few beings in the world who understand rightly the character of God. The great majority of mankind do not comprehend anything, either that which is past or that which is to come, as it respects their relationship to God....
> If men do not comprehend the character of God, they do not comprehend themselves....
> I want to ask this congregation, every man, woman and child, to answer the question in their own hearts, what kind of a being God is?...
> I am going to inquire after God; for I want you all to know Him, and to be familiar with Him [*History of the Church*, 6:303, 305]

Joseph also suggests that answering what kind of being God is will "peradventure, from this time henceforth occupy your attention" (Ibid. 6:303). That means a vast amount of time, thought, and sacrifice is required to comprehend the true nature of God.

To gain self-knowledge, then to view it beside God's vast intelligence, produces humility. It also develops faith, which eventually extends mere belief into pure knowledge. "The first fundamental is belief—with Latter-day Saints a knowledge—in the existence of a personal God." (David O. McKay, *Conference Report*, April 1934, 22-23)

We are promised, "He that keepeth his commandments receiveth truth and light, until he is glorified in truth and knoweth all things" (D&C 93:28). Eventually, the "day shall come when [we] shall comprehend even God" (D&C 88:49). How wonderful to know we can think, speak, and act in the same way God does!

Be Perfect

After Jesus's death and ascension to heaven, He appeared to the Nephites, whom He admonished, "Therefore I would that ye should be perfect even as I, or your Father who is in heaven is perfect" (3 Nephi 12:48). The prophet Lorenzo Snow expounded upon this verse:

> We may think that we cannot live up to the perfect law, that the work of perfecting ourselves is too difficult. This may be true in part, but the fact still remains that it is a command of the Almighty to us and we cannot ignore it. When we experience trying moments, then is the time for us to avail ourselves of the great privilege of calling upon the Lord for strength and understanding, intelligence and grace by which we can overcome the weakness of the flesh....
>
> The Latter-day Saints expect to arrive at this state of perfection; we expect to become as our Father and God, fit and worthy children to dwell in his presence; we expect that when the Son of God shall appear, we shall receive our bodies renewed and glorified, and that these vile bodies will be changed and become like unto his glorious body (see Phil. 3:210). These are our expectations. [*Journal of Discourses*, vol. 20, 187-192]

How glorious to be promised that our "bodies will be changed and become like unto his." But we must be patient, like tulip bulbs awaiting spring. Though we may struggle to sprout between chilling storms, our growth will be steadier and straighter as our hearts, minds, and spirits become more purified. With consistent, faithful effort, we can improve to the point that "in [us] is no darkness at all" (1 John 1:5).

That task should not be postponed. It must begin today. At this instant. I may have a panic attack just thinking about it! Now, at this very moment, is barely soon enough for me to stretch more diligently toward perfection.

Conclusion

With all the Father and Son have done and are doing to save me and you, it's important to show our gratitude. Their only desire is to elevate us to heavenly realms. So I frequently must ask myself if I'm exerting enough effort to know and become like the Father and Son. I am intrigued by the following words of Elder Bruce R. McConkie:

> It is one thing to know about God and another to know him. We know about him when we learn that he is a personal being in whose image man is created; when we learn that the Son is in the express image of his Father's person; when we learn that both the Father and the Son possess certain attributes and powers. But we know them, in the sense of gaining eternal life, when we enjoy and experience the same things they do. To know God is to think what he thinks, to feel what he feels, to have the power he possesses, to comprehend the truths he understands, and to do what he does. Those who know God become like him, and have his kind of life, which is eternal life. [*Doctrinal New Testament Commentary*, 1:762]

I can never know too much about God the Father and His Son Jesus Christ. "Behold, who can glory too much in the Lord? Yea, who can say too much of his great power, and of his mercy, and of his long-suffering towards the children of men?" (Alma 26:16). With each morsel of increased spiritual knowledge, I can better love and serve my Savior. Each stride anyone makes toward celestial glory will be rewarded.

Elder Neal A. Maxwell said, "The more we know of Jesus, the more we will love Him. The more we know of Jesus, the more we will trust Him. The more we know of Jesus, the more we will want to be like Him and to be with Him by becoming the manner of men and women that He wishes us to be (see 3 Nephi 27:27). ["Plow in Hope" *Ensign*, May 2001, 60]

For additional insight, see the following:

- Gordon B. Hinckley, "The Father, Son, and Holy Ghost," *Ensign*, November 1986, pp. 49-51.

Jesus spake unto them, saying,
Be of good cheer;
it is I; be not afraid.
Matthew 14:27

Be Of Good Cheer

When we strive to know the Father and Son, we learn of Their divine love and desire for us to return to Them. We feel comfort in the words: "be of good cheer, for I will lead you along. The kingdom is yours and the blessings thereof are yours, and the riches of eternity are yours" (D&C 78:18). With the promise of eternal life, toward which the Lord leads the willing of heart, we have every reason to be of good cheer.

On a snowy afternoon years ago, I drove to the elementary school to pick up my two younger sons. While watching the chilly departure of children from the building, I glimpsed a brother and sister walking together. The boy was lanky and tall, perhaps a sixth grader, who tightly held hands with a small girl, probably a kindergartener. The brother supported his sister through snowdrifts, steadied her over slippery spots, and guided her safely between the waiting vehicles. Then he opened the door of their Suburban, helped her onto the high seat, and made sure she was buckled in before he went to climb in the other side.

How like something our elder brother Jesus would do for us! Though not tangibly holding our hand, He helps us navigate through snowdrifts of adversity and traverse the slippery spots of doubt and fear. He guides us around the traffic of temptation, then snugly buckles us into the gospel of truth so we might safely return home. Our task is to remember He is always there, so we can fearlessly follow His beckoning.

Be Not Afraid

Fear is the opposite of faith, which is why scriptures repeatedly admonish "fear not" and "be not afraid." One familiar account is found in Matthew, chapter 14, paraphrased below:

The day was far from ordinary. Jesus fed five thousand people with a few loaves and fishes. He taught them, healed many, then lovingly sent the multitude home to ponder His words. As evening approached, He asked His disciples to go before Him across the Sea of Galilee, while He went alone to a mountain to pray.

During His prayer, Jesus undoubtedly felt the sting of wind that thrashed the tall grasses and whirled chaff into the air. He probably smelled the dampness of approaching rain as clouds billowed to obscure the moon and stars. Even from where He knelt on the hillside, He heard the churning waves upon the sea, threatening the ship that carried His disciples. Yet it was far into the night when Jesus arose from His prayer, tightened His cloak around Himself, and neared the seashore.

> But the ship was now in the midst of the sea, tossed with waves: for the wind was contrary.
> And in the fourth watch of the night, Jesus went unto them, walking on the sea.
> And when the disciples saw him walking on the sea, they were troubled, saying, It is a spirit; and they cried out for fear.
> But straightway Jesus spake unto them, saying, Be of good cheer; it is I; be not afraid. [Matthew 14:24-27]

Though fierce waves crashed upon the small ship, the Master's words diminished the disciples' fears. And Peter called out, "Lord, if it be thou, bid me come unto thee upon the water" (v. 28).

Jesus spoke but one word: "Come" (v. 29).

Had I been Peter, I would likely have changed my mind and stayed in the ship. I'd have kept a white-knuckled grip on the side or hugged the center mast—anything to stay on the ship in the midst of the thunderous storm.

How hard it may seem to come unto Christ, though He beckons to us amid the engulfing waves of worldly fears! Surrounded by tumultuous trials, we strain to hear His reassuring voice: "In the world ye shall have tribulation: but be of good cheer; I have overcome the world" (John 16:33).

That day on the Sea of Galilee, Peter exercised extreme faith, came down out of the ship, and actually began to walk on the water toward his friend Jesus Christ. But the wind was boisterous, tossing waves and splashing Peter. The wild scene terrified him. When fear supplanted his faith, he failed to focus on Christ. Peter then began to sink in the sea, and cried out, "Lord, save me" (Matthew 14:30).

"Immediately, Jesus stretched forth his hand," caught hold of his friend, and lifted him out of danger. Surely, Peter's heart ached to hear the Master's words, "O thou of little faith, wherefore didst thou doubt?" (Matthew 14:31)

The two of them settled in the ship, while those aboard marveled because the storm miraculously ceased. The disciples probably brought blankets to wrap around Peter. Perhaps he berated himself for his shattered faith. "Why did I fear?" he may have chided. "Despite the fierce storm, with the Son of God so near, how could I have lost faith? If only I had kept my thoughts focused on Jesus, then I would not have faltered and let myself sink, no matter how turbulent the waves."

Our own experiences may parallel Peter's. When the dark storms and trials of life blow in, and insurmountable waves crash around us, we must overcome fear with perfect faith in Christ. He is not merely an ethereal being. He is our personal Savior, who comprehends all the storms that arise in our lives. If our thoughts are steadily fastened on the Lord, His Spirit will whisper, "Be of good cheer; it is I; be not afraid."

Do Not Get Lost

Amid the dry, desert landscape, south of Escalante, Utah, is a mini Grand Canyon called Coyote Gulch. Looking up from the depths of the gulch, one sees two-hundred-foot sandstone walls, carved by countless centuries of rushing water. Today there remains just a shallow stream, averaging two inches in depth and twelve feet in width. The spring-fed creek roves for about ten miles until it joins the Escalante River, which flows into Lake Powell.

During the 1980s I helped chaperone our ward Young Men and Young Women on several backpacking treks to Coyote Gulch. Because of the massive sandstone cliffs, there are very few safe entrances into the deep gorge. On two of our trips, we rapelled with ropes over the cliff midway along the gulch, near the Jacob Hamblin Arch. Another journey took our group down the eastern most trail, through a slit in the cliffs, then on a descending trail called the "sand bar."

Only once did I travel the western-most trail, which begins at Red Canyon and meanders many miles into the gulch. Tagging along with some friends and their children during a May weekend, I had left my own four children and husband Glenn at home. This was my Mothers' Day present, to go on a short trip without my usual family obligations. My kids were probably happy to have me gone for a few days. No more enduring my experimental recipes like orange Jell-O with shredded carrots and cheddar cheese—at least the colors blended well. My husband would probably give in to the kids' cravings for carry-out pizza or meals at McDonalds.

With a group of fifteen, from adults to children, I began backpacking into the Red Canyon headwaters, where the tiny stream gradually widenened with water seeping from the cliff walls. At ninety degrees Fahrenheit, the desert air seemed more tolerable with our splashing steps in the water. Before long, the cliffs steepened to shade us from the relentless sun.

Moving at a slow pace, with parents shepherding their children, I grew bored, as did a trio of their adolescent sons. When the three teens strode faster to outpace the group, I hastened to follow them. For about a mile I trod behind the lanky boys, who seemed unaware of their weighty backpacks. On the other hand—or should I say the other foot?—I soon discovered that my own bulky backpack was slowing me down. I should have restrained myself from packing so many "comforts of home." No matter my desire to maintain a rapid stride, the gap between me and the three boys widened. I simply could not keep up.

At that point I should have reconsidered why I'd followed teenagers in the first place. Kids in that age bracket are not known for good judgment. Obviously my judgment was just as unsound. While their youthful legs soon took them out of sight, I felt somewhat relieved to set my own pace in the shallow stream. I put a cassette tape into my Walkman and sang with it while insects hummed beside me in the arid climate. Red sand and water oozed into my shabby shoes as I splashed along. During former treks to this gulch, I'd discovered whatever I wore was permanently stained by the iron-oxide-infused soil.

The narrow river serpentined in broad curves through an ever-increasing height of sandstone walls. To shorten the distance of the snaking streambed, I cut across sandbars and rocky outcroppings. Occasionally, I stopped to gawk at various cacti, trees, and other meager vegetation on the banks. I watched squirrels scamper across fallen logs and rabbits hop beneath scanty bushes for shelter. Twice the whoosh of jet aircraft overhead caught my attention.

Enjoying the toil of my muscles and bones through these serene scenes of nature, I lost track of time. Little did I know, I was also losing track of the correct route.

I reached a fork in the creek and wondered which one to take. Then it dawned on me that I was going upstream instead of downstream. I had no idea how long I had hiked the wrong way. The word *"LOST!"* loomed loudly in my mind. *Why does there have to be opposition in all things?*

Initially I worried that in cutting the corners I'd climbed out of Coyote Gulch and was stranded in another of the nearby gorges. I envisioned my friends going back to Salt Lake without me on Mother's Day to tell my family they'd searched for me in vain.

Lost, lost, lost, echoed in my mind. *Brain cells come, and brain cells go. But bad decisions are always available.*

After my initial panic subsided, I dropped to my knees and pled for guidance from the Lord. Perhaps you, too, have offered one of those desperate prayers: *Please, Father, can you help me solve this dilemma? And maybe forget about the countless other times I've begged for mercy? Any chance that I could get an answer quickly and not have to wait for Thy timetable? I need help now!*

Being an optimist, I quickly regenerated my hope for divine direction, and I leaped to my feet with renewed determination. Making an about-face, I hastened downstream toward what I thought was the correct creek bed.

For thirty minutes I hiked alone with my heart beating louder than the music in my ears. Forty minutes, then fifty, then an entire hour passed. I didn't pass any familiar landscapes. Nor did I find another human. I would have been relieved to see a ghost or demon, just to not feel so alone! How I longed for assurance that I was correctly headed toward the Jacob Hamblin Arch.

After one hour and fifteen minutes, a young couple appeared around a bend. I nearly hugged them both! They said the arch I sought was a half-mile downstream. With renewed energy, I quickened my pace and soon arrived at the pre-arranged campsite. The trio of boys I had earlier followed were resting on their sleeping bags near the famed arch. I found a quiet spot, rolled out my bag, then knelt upon it and breathed a prayer of thanks.

Needless to say, being lost in the wilderness brings a horrendous feeling of insecurity. Scriptures sometimes refer to our lives on earth as a wilderness from which the Lord calls us toward eternal life. "This church have I established and called forth out of the wilderness" (D&C 33:5).

The prophet Lehi related a dream of being in the wilderness, then later he partook of fruit from the glorious tree of life.

I saw in my dream, a dark and dreary wilderness.
And it came to pass that I saw a man, and he was dressed in a white robe; and he came and stood before me.

And ... he spake unto me, and bade me follow him.

And ... as I followed him I beheld myself that I was in a dark and dreary waste.

And after I had traveled for the space of many hours in darkness, I began to pray unto the Lord that he would have mercy on me, according to the multitude of his tender mercies.

And ... after I had prayed unto the Lord ...

I beheld a tree, whose fruit was desirable to make one happy" (1 Nephi 8:4–10).

Blessed by the tender mercies of the Lord, Lehi partook of the fruit, which filled him with joy. Immediately he wanted his family to enjoy the pure fruit (see vv. 11-12). Only after journeying for many hours in the dark and dreary wilderness was Lehi prepared for the reward of the pure white fruit from the tree of life.

Lehi's dream was symbolic of his family's lengthy travels to reach the blessings of the Promised Land. More importantly, it represented his individual journey, like our own, through the wilderness of mortality to reach eternal life. All through the wilderness, Lehi followed a man dressed in a white robe, just as we should follow Jesus Christ through our earthly sojourn until we reach the tree of life. It's up to each of us to cheerfully do all that we can to achieve salvation. "Therefore,... let us cheerfully do all things that lie in our power; and then may we stand still, with the utmost assurance, to see the salvation of God" (D&C 123:17.

A Disciple of Christ

Want to tackle something new in your life? You could try out to be an astronaut. Climb Mount Everest. Audition for the Metropolitan Opera. Or perhaps you could fully commit to being a Disciple of Christ, who said, "He that receiveth my law and doeth it, the same is my disciple" (D&C 41:5).

Disciple comes from the same root word as *discipline.* Unfortunately, we have come to think of discipline as a punishment. Actually, it means to teach or instruct. Webster's dictionary defines discipline as "training or experience that corrects, molds, strengthens, or perfects especially the mental faculties or moral character." A disciple is defined as "one who receives instruction from another; one who accepts the doctrines of another and assists in spreading or implementing them." Therefore, it is not enough to merely receive and accept doctrine. I must also utilize it in my life and spread it to others, but not in the same manner as I shared a flu virus last winter.

Sometimes we call ourselves, "Mormons;" yet in our hearts we are actually disciples and Latter-day Saints. Webster's definition of *saint* is also interesting: "from the root word sanctus, meaning sacred, pure, holy, consecrated."

I can readily see how those words might apply to other Latter-day Saints. But myself? Maybe I shouldn't mention the day my bishop asked me to be the nursery leader, and I said, "Can I change that calling for what's behind door number two?" While I was there I said, "Bishop, that reminds me. Have you thought about making sacrament meeting more entertaining? Perhaps you could try a game show format."

Where was I? Oh, yes, a saint should be pure and holy and consecrated. Okay, so I'm a long way from achieving qualities of sainthood. But I shall keep trying.

Decades ago, when television was not as advanced as in today's world, transmission troubles occurred frequently. A specific pattern would show on the screen while the announcer said, "Please stand by. We are having technical difficulties." I remember that occurred one afternoon when my three-year-old son was watching TV. Without hesitation, he leaped off the couch and stood next to the television. "Okay," he said, "I'm standing by."

Have you ever been drowning in trials and needed someone to "stand by" and support you? Often it's a close friend or relative who lends a listening ear or provides a gentle hug. Always remember that Jesus is also near, providing words of encouragement: "Be of good cheer, and do not fear, for I the Lord am with you, and will stand by you" (D&C 68:6).

When we stand beside Christ as His true disciples, we know He is always available to help us overcome the technical difficulties of life, whether temporal or spiritual. Our tasks is to remember He is there and call on Him while He is near.

Children of God

One reason to be of good cheer is that we are children of God. Though much of the world's population doesn't grasp that concept, Latter-day Saints believe every person on earth is our spiritual brother or sister. I'm grateful for this verse inviting us to joyfully share the gospel with them all: "Let thy heart be of good cheer before my face; and thou shalt bear record of my name, not only unto the Gentiles, but also unto the Jews; and thou shalt send forth my word unto the ends of the earth" (D&C 112:4).

Travels have taken me to many places on the globe, where I've been blessed to sense a kinship with the people I encounter. I'm lucky to be a people-lover and people-watcher. Recently I visited parts of China, a country with over a billion people, and I felt sad that I would never get to know them personally. But I felt more sorrow to think that many of them will never know Jesus Christ until after their deaths. Yet each one is vitally important in the eyes of our Heavenly Father.

In the year 1993 I took my first trip to the Holy Land. While at the temple mount in Jerusalem, I wrote in my journal about feeling akin to my spiritual siblings at that site:

I stand shoulder to shoulder amongst Jewish women at the "Wailing Wall." I overhear their absorbing prayers, hoping to invoke God's blessings in answer to their needs. Many sway back and forth, flooded with emotion. I see tears flow down their cheeks with their earnest pleadings to God. How I yearn to embrace them, one by one, and soothe their troubled souls! I sense their depth of piety and their desire to connect with powers On High.

There is a sacredness here. These women are touched by the Spirit in ways they might not fully understand. But I know the Light of Christ dwells in each heart. Perhaps some of them pray for the Messiah to appear and change the course of their lives. How sad that they don't know He has already come! How unfortunate they don't know the blessings of His atonement and resurrection.

Summoning all the energy of His soul and bleeding from every pore, Jesus Christ took upon himself the burdens of this entire world. Surely in all our earth's history, this was the most poignant, pivotal event of all time.

Yesterday I stood quietly in the Garden of Gethsemane to contemplate what I might do to repay the Lord's sacrifice in my behalf. My meditation was repeatedly disrupted by the commotion of the world: horns honked, motors hummed, plumes of black smoke spewed from roaring busses, and people called out their wares to sell. Life in Jerusalem went on as usual, without anyone pausing to ponder about that crucial moment in Gethsemane.

Millennia ago, on that sacred evening when Jesus prayed in profound agony, the majority of Jews went about their normal lives, unaware of His infinite sacrifice. They never knew the depth of His love as He suffered to pay the ransom for us all.

The Reality of Jesus Christ

President Spencer W. Kimball offered his reflections about how many people at the time of Christ failed to recognize Him as the Son of God:

I wondered how many tens of thousands did hear Christ's voice, felt an inner twinge of heart, wanted to follow, felt impelled to do his will, but waited, paused, lingered, postponed, procrastinated....

How many heard his sermons on the mount and were pricked in their hearts, but stopped to eat food and sleep and work and do other things, and failed to heed?

Numerous have jostled him in narrow streets of Jerusalem, and turned around and looked the second time at him whom they had touched, but went on their way to daily tasks and missed their opportunity.

How many heard the story of his walking on the water but were too busy with their selling fish in the market or herding sheep or harvesting grain to ask the vital reasons and fathom the deep powers?

How many saw him hanging there upon the cross and saw only wood beams and nails and flesh and blood and made no effort to penetrate the purposes and the reasons—how one could choose to die such an ignominious death,... what it was that could cause a person to give himself for others and make no effort to escape? [*Hidden Wedges*, 21]

There are days I yearn to hop in a time travel machine and go to the Holy Land when Christ was living there. I wish I could personally observe him interacting with the people—old, young, rich, poor, sick, healthy, ruler, commoner. How blessed they were, though many never recognized who this magnificent God/man was. Sometimes I wonder, had I lived in the meridian of time, if I would have been one of Christ's humble followers, or an unobservant bystander, or perhaps one of His persecutors. Those who do recognize Jesus Christ as our Savior and Redeemer are blessed by His comforting words: "be of good cheer, little children; for I am in your midst, and I have not forsaken you" (D&C 61:36).

Though an eternal being, Jesus has a tangible body of flesh and bones that experienced day-to-day life on earth. The winds blew through His hair, the rains fell on His face, and the sun shined warmly upon His shoulders. His hands were skilled at carpentry and at blessing the sick or raising the dead. As He trod the dusty trails of Palestine, dirt and pebbles soiled His sandaled feet. No wonder it was a customary courtesy to wash travelers' feet.

Jesus had a close connection with the earth that He created, and He used His observations of nature to teach the people in parables. The words He spoke were carried on currents of air that still circulate the earth today. Because I like to think of Jesus in tangible terms, I was grateful to feel His reality in these words:

It being the usual custom of Roman Governors to [advise]
the Senate and people of such material things as happened in
their respective provinces, in the days of the Emperor Tiberias
Caesar, Publius Lentulus, President of Judea, wrote the
following epistle to the Senate concerning the Savior:

Conscript Fathers: There has appeared in these our days, a man
of great virtue, named Jesus Christ, who is yet living amongst
us, and of the people is accepted for a prophet of truth, but his
disciples call him the Son of God. He raiseth the dead and
cureth all manner of diseases—a man of stature, somewhat
tall and comely, with a very reverent countenance, such as the
beholders may both love and fear; his hair of the color of a
filbert full ripe, and plain to his ears, but thence downwards
it is more orient, curling and waving about his shoulders; in
the midst of his head is a seam or partition of his hair after the
manner of the Nazarites; his forehead plain and very delicate;
his face without spot or wrinkle, beautiful with a lovely red; his
nose and mouth so formed that nothing can be reprehended;
his beard thickish in color like the hair of his head, not very
long but forked; his look innocent and mature; his eyes grey,
clear, and quick; in reproving he is terrible; in admonishing,
courteous and fair spoken; pleasant in conversation, mixed
with gravity. It cannot be remembered that any have seen
him laugh, but many have seen him weep. In proportion of
body most excellent; his hands and arms most delectable to
behold; in speaking, very temperate, modest and wise. A man
of singular beauty surpassing the children of men. [Rudger
Clawson, Conference Report, April 1927, 77]

Whether this document is truly from an ancient record or
not, I appreciate this description of the Messiah's appearance
and demeanor. One line seems quite meaningful: "It cannot be
remembered that any have seen Him laugh, but many have seen
Him weep." How gracious our Redeemer was to voluntarily suffer
in our behalf. He chose to die and atone for our sins that we, like
Him, might live again. As scriptures attest, He was "despised and

rejected of men; a man of sorrows, and acquainted with grief.... Surely he hath borne our griefs, and carried our sorrows" (Isaiah 53:3-4).

Conclusion

Because of the Redeemer's sacrifice and Atonement, we can be healed of the sins and sorrows of this world. It is as if He says to each of us, as He did to the man with palsy, "be of good cheer; thy sins be forgiven thee" (Matthew 9:2).

If we repent and choose Christ's way of life, we will not anguish as He did for all mankind (see D&C 19:15-19). What a privilege and blessing He has provided for us to be of good cheer! "Therefore, cheer up your hearts, and remember that ye are free to act for yourselves—to choose the way of everlasting death or the way of eternal life" (2 Nephi 10:23).

As a teenager in the 1960's, I recall when a young man sat beside me in seminary class and showed me the latest *Time* magazine. Emblazoned on its cover were the words "God Is Dead." A sudden pang clenched my chest as I considered the headline. Yet my adolescent testimony recoiled only for a fraction of a second. Somehow I knew the opposite: God lives! That day our seminary teacher provided a memorable discussion to reinforce our faith.

Much later in my life, I read a magazine article titled "Can We Be Good Without God?" The premise was that the world commonly consists of men and women of integrity. Whether religious or not, much of earth's population is honest in behavior, kind to neighbors, and attentive to their families' needs. Even those living in poverty show compassion for their fellow beings. Unfortunately, much goodness is overlooked. Though we hear occasional stories of "Mother Teresas" or "Nelson Mandelas," our daily news accounts rarely report the frequent and courageous good deeds of men and women. The article summarized by declaring that people are inherently good with or without God's interfering. But my question remains, is "good" truly good enough?

I believe God's children must become pure and sanctified by overcoming the world, in the same manner as Jesus did. Every moment of His time, thought, and energy was to build His Father's Kingdom. Then He sacrificed His life and atoned for all of us that we might become pure and sanctified.

A few days ago I picked up a bottle of drinking water, and the label read, "purified by reverse osmosis." I should look into that procedure. Sounds scientific and perhaps easier than sacrificing my whole life to become like Jesus. Maybe the purifying process of "reverse osmosis" could be done while I'm slouching in my lounge chair and watching TV. Do you think? Probably not. Though it may cause some heartache and suffering, there's really just one way to follow Christ toward exaltation. Only by emulating Him, can we overcome the tribulations of the world and receive eternal peace.

Jesus said, "These things I have spoken unto you, that in me ye might have peace. In the world ye shall have tribulation: but be of good cheer; I have overcome the world" (John 16:33).

With thoughts of Jesus Christ filling our hearts, we have no need to fear and every reason to be of good cheer. Just as He calmed the disciples' anxiety amid the tempest on the Sea of Galilee, He can also quiet troubled souls with the reassurance, "Be of good cheer; it is I; be not afraid" (Matthew 14:27).

For additional insight see the following:

- Spencer W. Kimball, "Jesus of Nazareth," *Ensign*, Dec. 1980, 3- 9.
- Patricia T. Holland, *A Quiet Heart*, Salt Lake City, Bookcraft, 2000.

But who may abide the day of his coming,
and who shall stand when he appeareth?
for he is like a refiner's fire . . .
Malachi 3:2

Refiner's  Fire

It is said that those who will burn at the "great and dreadful day of the Lord" (Mal. 4:5) are those who are not on fire now!

So how dynamic is your spiritual fire? Are you ignited with testimony? Flaming with faith? Burning with love for God? Ablaze with joy and rejoicing in the gospel of Jesus Christ? Kindled with enthusiasm as a member-missionary? Flaring with forgiveness toward those who despitefully use you and persecute you? All fired up about consecrating yourself to the Lord? Inflamed with desire to become more like the Father and Son?

Rarely can a human be constantly "on fire." After all, we do have to sleep. And at times we may feel drained—spiritually, mentally, emotionally, or physically. Amid self-checks and repair attempts, we may discover we've sizzled into lukewarm embers.

When my spirituality fades, it often takes more than one mere match to relight it—sometimes a bonfire is required. Then I must remember it will be "miserable to dwell with a holy and just God, under a consciousness of your filthiness before him,...

"For behold, when ye shall be brought to see your nakedness before God, and also the glory of God, and the holiness of Jesus

Christ, it will kindle a flame of unquenchable fire upon you"
(Mormon 9:4–5). *Unquenchable fire.* Sounds like descriptions of hell.
Of course, we don't have to understand the physics of hell to be
sent there.

Dealing With Life's Dragons

During lunch with a friend, I noticed she seemed joyless. I asked
what was wrong. Rather than naming a specific difficulty, she said,
"Life is easier when I know what dragon I'm dealing with." Like
many of us, she had endured numerous trials, including the death
of a six-week-old baby. However, that day at lunch, she could not
pinpoint a precise problem that made her life miserable.

Pondering my own trials, I softly said, "The dragon you deal
with is always yourself." In every phase of life—young or old, rich
or poor, married or single—the dragon you deal with is always
yourself. It's mostly a matter of attitude, perception, and reaction
to life's surprises. God has given us agency to choose an optimistic
outlook or to select the worst possible scenario.

Negativity can create a dragon-like response within us, which
we are hesitant to confront. The devil also tosses in his "fiery
darts" (1 Nephi 15:24) to further thwart us with discouragement.
If we're not careful to keep our negative thoughts from inflating,
that self-imposed dragon can become our own worst enemy. Facing
a ferocious fire-breathing creature is fearful and frightening. It
makes a person feel rather small. Then, to discover the dragon is
self-inflicted may make us feel more depressed.

However, I believe a dragon within us, particularly one that
snorts fire, can be a blessing. When viewed through spiritual eyes,
we might see it's nothing more than the Refiner's fire, purifying
our human nature. "And I will ... refine them as silver is refined,
and will try them as gold is tried: they shall call on my name, and
I will hear them" (Zechariah 13:9).

Perhaps that day at lunch I could have said to my friend, "You're
just at that age. You're having hot flashes." More likely, I should
have said, "Watch out! It's the Refiner's fire! Turn on your garden
hose and run like lightning to escape!"

Yet no one can outrun God, who said, "Behold,... I have chosen thee in the furnace of affliction" (Isaiah 48:10). It's best to survive our scalding trials by turning on the air conditioner, or, in religious terms, by turning toward Christ. The Lord knows what is best. Though some people question why He created scorpions, He does not make errors in judgment. When we choose to let the Savior sanctify us, He will help us qualify for celestial glory.

Be Open To The Refiner's Fire

One day in late March, I walked through my neighborhood to enjoy the refreshing spring scenery. Rounding a corner, I neared a pine tree and heard noises from high in the boughs. Crackle, crack. Snap, snap, pop, crackle, pop! The sound made me think of extremely intent Rice Krispies. Pushing aside a sudden hunger, since I'd not yet eaten breakfast, I stepped closer to the trunk and peered up into the dense needles. I expected to see a squirrel or bird, but no critters came into view. The snapping and crackling continued intermittently. Shifting position, I still did not find any cause for the noise. Across the street stood another evergreen, so I traversed the warm asphalt to again hear "crack-crraaaak, snap-snaaaap." No wildlife made the sound, nor could I discern any other reason for it.

After gawking upward for a several minutes, my neck stiffened, so I decided to move onward through the neighborhood. Approaching our church house, I spied a series of evergreens in front of it. From the nearest trees, I heard the now-familiar snapping and popping. When I glanced at a bough overhead, the answer crystallized: a pinecone! That's what had crackled! An intent study of other cones on the tree seemed to confirm my theory: As the bright sunrays warmed them, the pinecones began to stretch and snap. Then the little blades on each cone cracked and widened, and tiny seeds fluttered to the ground.

I circled one tree to locate a low branch from which I could take a pinecone as a reminder. That's when I realized the cones on the north side of the tree were still tightly closed. None had been in a position for the sunshine to warm them and help them snap, crackle, and pop open. How intriguing!

That afternoon I visited the public library to study about pinecones. There I verified my theory that pinecones do open with warmth—some only from the intense heat of forest fires. That's why evergreens, rather than deciduous trees, are usually first to sprout from the ground after wildfires.

During 1989, devastating fires swept through Yellowstone National Park. Most of the incinerated trees were lodgepole pines, which have cones that explode in fierce heat. The ravishing blaze consumed the old decaying and diseased trees. Then, in the aftermath of what seemed complete destruction, renewed life germinated from the pinecones that burst open and spread their seeds. Three years after the fire, when our family held a reunion in Yellowstone, we found delight in the thousands of tiny pine trees, less than two feet tall, that had sprung up in the fire scars.

I have experimented with putting tightly closed pinecones in my oven at a low temperature. It takes but a few minutes for them to snap, crackle, and pop open. Don't try this yourself unless you put them on foil so the seeds and sap don't make a mess of your oven. Not only do the warm pinecones give off a nice aroma, but also when they're broadly opened, they look much nicer on display than the tightly closed cones.

An open pinecone has shared its life, given of itself to nourish the earth. But one that fails to unwrap its seeds is useless in the natural world. Likewise, it is said that "a person completely wrapped up in himself makes a small package." When we open our hearts to let the Refiner's fire burn away our impurities, we become more fruitful and better able to nourish the world around us.

Willingly Submit

Don't go asking for adversity. Don't ever say, "Fire at will!" Not when it's God's will we're talking about. That would be like instead of taking a dive, doing a back flip and hitting your head on the diving board. Believe me, trials will appear suddenly. Boy! Will they ever! It's part of the plan. You agreed to be tested here.

Remember reading that in the small print on the contract you signed before coming to earth?

When faced with afflictions and hardships, just phone home, 1-800-HUMBLED, and God will be there. He'll know you are now willing to submit to His purifying power. Then He can endow you with added power to accomplish His purposes on earth.

Submitting our will to the Father, as our Savior did, gives us empowerment directly from God. It brings humility, renders peace, offers hope, provides courage to meet life's adversities, opens hearts to love, and strengthens testimonies of the Lord's power of redemption. Jesus Chirst set the supreme example of meekness and submissiveness. His Atonement was the most transcendent event in all history. His words shall ring throughout time and eternity as the most profound ever spoken, "Not my will, but thine, be done" (Luke 22:42).

Distress and adversity are not meant to cripple us. They are like fertilizer to help us grow. Have you noticed how some weeds, like twisting morning glory vines, blossom into the loveliest flowers? Just as weeds can become a thing of beauty in some people's eyes, adversity can become a blessing in humble, righteous souls. Remember these lines that may have been cross-stitched and framed on your grandmother's wall? "When life gives you lemons, make lemonade." "When life gives you scraps, make quilts."

At times, the Refiner's fire may seem harsh and overwhelming. At least it doesn't smell bad like burning refuse at the city dump. Might as well endure the pain and allow your spirit to be purified. Then, when you get to heaven, you won't be court martialed for going AWOL in the midst of life's battles.

Remember God's words to Joseph Smith during his afflictions in the Liberty Jail—isn't that an ironic name for a prison? "Know thou, my son, that all these things shall give thee experience, and shall be for thy good.

"The Son of Man hath descended below them all. Art thou greater than he?" (D&C 122:7-8).

One astute latter-day apostle said the same thing in an analogous way: "We should not complain about our own life's not being a rose garden when we remember who wore the crown of thorns!" (Neal A. Maxwell, "Overcome ... Even As I Also Overcame," *Ensign*, May 1987, 72)

Baptism Of Fire

In addition to the Refiner's fire, receiving the Holy Ghost is referred to as a baptism of fire (see D&C 19:31). Jesus declared, "And whoso cometh unto me with a broken heart and a contrite spirit, him will I baptize with fire and with the Holy Ghost" (3 Nephi 9:20).

The Holy Ghost is a sanctifier, helping us become pure, perfect, and prepared to dwell with our Father in the celestial kingdom. "Repent,... and be baptized in my name, that ye may be sanctified by the reception of the Holy Ghost, that ye may stand spotless before me at the last day" (3 Nephi 27:20).

When I looked up "spotless" on my computer thesaurus, these words appeared: speckless, spick-and-span, scoured, scrubbed, cleansed, immaculate. Okay. God wants us to arrive at His throne clean and pure—uncontaminated, and unpolluted—despite our experiences on earth.

Allowing the Holy Ghost to burn away our impure thoughts and actions may entail acute pain. But we can survive it, thanks to the Atonement of Christ. Purification is not possible without His sacrifice, which enables the Spirit to cleanse us. Joseph Smith explained that sanctification and exaltation are not merely life-long goals, but eternity-long processes.

When you climb up a ladder, you must begin at the bottom, and ascend step by step, until you arrive at the top; and so it is with the principles of the Gospel—you must begin with the first, and go on until you learn all the principles of exaltation. But it will be a great while after you have passed through the veil [died] before you will have learned them. It is not all to be comprehended in this world; it will be a great work to learn our salvation and exaltation even beyond the grave" [*Teachings of the Prophet Joseph Smith*, 348]

Chastening from the Lord

When the Refiner's fire seems to cauterize my soul, I try to remember it's for my own good. Though it might feel harsh and painful, it is an act of love sent from God, who said, "despise not thou the chastening of the Lord,…

"For whom the Lord loveth he chasteneth,…

"Now no chastening for the present seemeth to be joyous, but grievous: nevertheless afterward it yieldeth the peaceable fruit of righteousness unto them which are exercised thereby" (Hebrews 12:5-6, 11).

I learned as a child about being chastened. Picture me as a tomboyish, rambunctious 13-year-old, playing baseball with my three younger brothers and some friends in our front yard. I was the pitcher, trying mightily to strike out those on the opposing team. During one of my pitches, I threw a fastball and squealed with delighted to see the batter swing and miss. However, my thrill dissolved into despair when the hurling baseball crashed through the basement window. I didn't dare move, but stood with my heart pounding and my mouth hanging open. Then one of my brothers stepped up, jabbed me in the side, and taunted me about paying for the broken window.

Paying is often the concern, though the actual money to cover a misdeed rarely equals the price paid in humiliation. Hence, my main concern was that my parents had heard the shattering glass and would come outside to scold me in front of my friends. Then I remembered my mother was away running Saturday afternoon errands, and I had last seen my father napping upstairs in the living room.

Even if he'd slept through the noise, I knew I must ascend the stairs and tell my father what I had done. The parallel, of course, is that someday I will have to ascend and report to my Father in Heaven what I have done on earth. By then it's too late to be read my rights: "You have the right to remain silent. You have the right to an attorney,… and so on." How much better off I'll be if I've learned to repent and accept the Lord's chastening as an opportunity for spiritual growth.

Verily, thus saith the Lord unto you whom I love, and whom I love I also chasten that their sins may be forgiven, for with the chastisement I prepare a way for their deliverance in all things out of temptation, and I have loved you—
Wherefore, ye must needs be chastened (D&C 95:1-2).

Chastening in the Last Days

As I said at the start of this chapter, "Those who will burn at the great and dreadful day of the Lord are those who are not on fire now!" Many prophets, ancient and modern, have foretold of fires, earthquakes, and other disasters that will occur before the Savior comes to reign on earth. Once in a while, I muster enough courage to examine these inspired prophecies. As the time draws nearer, I wonder if "once in a while" is often enough to prepare me to participate in positive ways.

Over a decade ago, October 1992 in general conference, Elder M. Russell Ballard addressed statistics of increasing natural disasters, unyielding diseases, and social unrest throughout the world. (See M. Russell Ballard, "The Joy of Hope Fulfilled," *Ensign*, November 1992, 31.) Additional statistics were mentioned during 1999 in a article from *Parade* magazine which often accompanies Sunday newspapers.

The year just past brought approximately 700 catastrophic natural disasters, which killed at least 50,000 people—making 1998 the most calamitous year on record, according to Munich Reinsurance, a German company that monitors natural disasters. Last year's total was three times the annual average for natural catastrophes during the 1960's.
Among the worst of this worst year: 240 windstorms, 170 floods and nine hurricanes (Mitch killed an estimated 9200 people [in Honduras and Nicaragua], cost $5 billion in uninsured losses and $150 million in insured losses). There was a typhoon in Japan, an earthquake in Afghanistan, a cyclone in India, mudslides in Italy, winter storms and a cold wave in

Europe, heat waves and forest fires in the U.S., Greece, and Brazil. ["1998: A Year of Disasters," *Parade*, 7 Feb. 1999]

Since that time, the tally of natural disasters shows increased destruction and deaths throughout the world. If the whole purpose of the Father is to save His children, why does He allow such calamities to plague the earth? No doubt the answer is to strip the earth of wickedness (see JS-Matthew. 1:31), and to purify the people who will receive Christ when He comes (see D&C 104:59).

Because the whole world must be cleansed before the New Jerusalem is built (see Ether 13:2-3), the United States will have its share of serious tribulations. One such disaster occurred the morning of 11 September 2001 when terrorists killed thousands by steering airplanes into the World Trade Towers and other sites. Sadly, catastrophic events of the future may injure or kill countless more—both wicked and righteous individuals.

None of us will forget the day after Christmas in 2004 when an earthquake in the Indian Ocean caused a terrifying tsunami. The ruinous waves clamored through island communities and beaches along southern Asia. Nearly 200,000 people died—not only Asians living there, but also many Europeans and Americans on holiday. Surely that confirms a Last Day's prophecy of the "waves of the sea heaving themselves beyond their bounds" (D&C 88:90).

Another south-Asian earthquake in 2005 left Pakistan in rubble and killed over 70,000 people. Most of us in America will recall the year 2005 as setting a record for hurricanes and tropical storms in the Atlantic and Gulf Coast areas. With the excessive number of storms, weather trackers ran out of the English alphabet then had to use the Greek alphabet to name them. With global warming, forecasters predict that 2006 may equal or exceed 2005's records.

News reporters are still talking about Hurricane Katrina that buried New Orleans in water on 29 August 2005. Then it continued its tirade, inundating other parts of Louisiana as well as Alabama and Mississippi. It took weeks and weeks for the water to recede enough for rescuers to uncover all the wounded and dead. In the meantime, thousands were left homeless, and refugees were sent to various locations in the United States. Many residents are still wondering how to begin new lives after losing all they owned.

A series of ravaging hurricanes, though not as destructive as Katrina, slammed into Florida during September of 2004. Hurricane Ivan veered toward the panhandle, where my brother, Jeff, and his family had a spacious two-story house. Ivan ripped through their neighborhood and left most of the homes unliveable. The photographs he emailed afterward stunned me.

As a member of the stake presidency, Jeff helped coordinate rescue efforts from their stake center in Pensacola. His wife and youngest son had driven north to safety in a rented a Suburban, crammed full of family records and other vital items. An older son and daughter were securely attending BYU.

Their eighteen-year-old son couldn't be persuaded he was in danger, so he remained alone at home to witness the destruction first-hand. Later, he would spend weeks volunteering his muscles for the vast cleanup efforts.

Upstairs asleep when Hurricane Ivan struck, my nephew was awakened by the violent noise. When the thrashing somewhat calmed, he ventured downstairs to view the damage. Though the second floor of their house was unscathed, a few feet of water remained on the first floor. The force of the murky liquid had overturned furniture, stripped plasterboard off the walls, and toppled bookcases, dumping their precious contents. The piano was no longer "upright" in the living room, and the refrigerator bobbed lamely in the kitchen. Their second family car had floated into a sideways position in the garage. Don't ask me how to get a car like that back in operating condition!

It's not like they could have driven anywhere. Fallen trees and debris from neighbors' homes had piled in the yards and streets to impede traffic. As water continued to recede, government officials and crews of volunteers moved into the area to assess damage and assist those in need of help.

A few days after the hurricane, Jeff's family was reunited at the stake center, where many residents of the area had taken shelter. For two weeks, their family lived in a tiny trailer, parked in the stake center's lot. Later they moved into a small two-bedroom house, where they stayed for several months. County agencies determined that their former home would have to be torn down, while the family suffered delayed and disappointing responses from insurance companies.

Hurricane Ivan was a financial disaster for my brother and his employer. Jeff's wife ventured daily to the ruined house to sift through anything that might be salvaged. Fortunately they were able to sell their property for the value of the land. Their family temporarily moved from the area, but they, like many victims of disaster, might soon return to live again where they'll always be concerned about another hurricane surging in.

These Things Must Come To Pass

While some contend that God could have prevented these hurricanes, tsunamis, earthquakes, and the 9/11 terror, those with eyes to see can recognize the many miracles and narrow escapes reported after such catastrophes. At times the Lord will calm a storm, while other times He lets the tempest rage, then calms His children.

Whether natural disasters or human-caused destruction, the Lord has provided warnings for those who attune their ears to hear: "Wherefore, the voice of the Lord is unto the ends of the earth, that all that will hear may hear.

"Prepare ye, prepare ye for that which is to come, for the Lord is nigh" (D&C 1:11-12).

Note the repetition of "prepare ye" to give it emphasis. Despite the upheavals in the Last Days, "if ye are prepared ye shall not fear" (D&C 38:30). God has urged us to "be not troubled: for all these things must come to pass" (Matthew 24:6).

When troubles do come, it's nice to recall the oft-repeated phrase from the Book of Mormon: "And it came to pass." Turbulence in the Last Days will not last forever. God is the great Overseer, who promises to abbreviate the times of distress. "And except those days should be shortened, there should no flesh be saved; but for the elect's sake those days shall be shortened" (Matthew 24:22).

Because Jesus Christ fashioned this earth, He has dominion over the land, the seas, and the heavens above. Better than any scientist, He comprehends the cataclysmic cycles of earthquakes, volcanos, hurricanes, typhoons, floods, tornados, mudslides, tsunamis, and so forth. More than once He used His divine power to calm the boisterous wind and waves on the Sea of Galilee with the simple command, "Peace, be still" (Mark 4:39).

Have you ever wanted to command the elements to "be still," as He did? Perhaps at a basketball game when the refs seem biased, or when you're trying to nap at a family reunion, or while you're at a petting zoo with children or grandchildren? It's frequently hard to be at peace amid the chaos and clamor of everyday life. During the Last Days, it will be crucial to have peace within our souls by remembering that God is in charge. "Therefore, let your hearts be comforted concerning Zion; for all flesh is in mine hands; be still and know that I am God" (D&C 101:16).

Unfortunately, prophecies foretell that more fearful events will come to pass before the millennium. Christ's words provide assurance to trust in Him during those days of unrest: "Peace I leave with you, my peace I give unto you: not as the world giveth, give I unto you. Let not your heart be troubled, neither let it be afraid" (John 14:27).

Watch Therefore

We must pay heed to the signs, as we're cautioned, "Watch therefore: for ye know not what hour your Lord doth come....

"Therefore be ye also ready: for in such an hour as ye think not the Son of man cometh" (Matthew 24:42, 44).

I've worried at the scripture that targets the trouble as a whirlwind starting at the Lord's house. "Behold, vengeance cometh speedily upon the inhabitants of the earth,... and as a whirlwind it shall come upon all the face of the earth, saith the Lord.

"And upon my house shall it begin, and from my house shall it go forth, saith the Lord" (D&C 112:24-25).

Those words call to mind the tornado that slashed through Salt Lake City in August 1999. Such cyclonic storms are extremely rare in Utah. That tornado made a swipe beside the Salt Lake Temple, the holy house of God. I wonder, is it literal that "upon [His] house it will begin"?

Another statement which concerns me is a prophecy that the constitution of the United States will hang by a thread. The revelation was attributed to Joseph Smith, as recounted by Brigham Young in this manner: "Will the Constitution be destroyed? No, it will be held inviolate by this people; and, as Joseph Smith said, 'The time will come when the destiny of the nation will hang upon a single thread. At that critical juncture, this people will step forth and save it from the threatened destruction.'" (*Journal of Discourses*, 7:15)

Joseph Smith did not use the word "constitution," but that the "*destiny of this nation* will hang upon a single thread." It can happen. Think of the U.S. Presidential elections in November 2000. The outcome was uncertain for three weeks because of "hanging chads" on the ballots. Whatever else may happen to make the destiny of the United States hang by a thread, it's clear that LDS Church members must be ready to rescue America. Perhaps we should be less worried about what happens in the White House and more focused on what occurs in the homes of Latter-day Saints.

In the opening address of October 1992 general conference, Gordon B. Hinckley quoted President Ezra Taft Benson, who was too feeble to speak for himself. "The kingdom of Heaven and the Kingdom of God on the earth will be combined together at Christ's coming—and that time is not far distant. How I wish we could get the vision of this work, the genius of it, and realize the nearness of that great event. I am sure it would have a sobering effect upon us if we realized what is before us" (*The Teachings of Ezra Taft Benson*, 19). President Benson gave additional insight in the following speech delivered to young adults in California:

God has saved for the final inning some of His strongest children, who will help bear off the kingdom triumphantly. That is where you come in, for you are the generation that must be prepared to meet your God....

Make no mistake about it—you are a marked generation. There has never been more expected of the faithful in such a short period of time as there is of us. Never before on the face of this earth have the forces of evil and the forces of good been as well organized.

Each day we personally make many decisions that show where our support will go. The final outcome is certain—the forces of righteousness will finally win. What remains to be seen is where each of us personally, now and in the future, will stand in this fight—and how tall we stand. Will we be true to our last-days, foreordained mission?" ["In His Steps," Church Educational System Devotional, Anaheim, CA, 8 Feb. 1987]

As part of the "forces of righteousness," what an impact Latter-day Saints can have around the globe! I'm reminded of the movie *Star Wars*, when Luke Skywalker rushes off to save the universe, and his mentor says, "May the force be with you." When we stand tall, as individuals and families, we truly can accomplish all that is expected of us in preparing the earth to receive the Lord. During every hour, minute, and second of our lives, we must be so ignited with faith that everything we do and say will testify of Christ.

In this book's prologue, I shared my dream about Jesus coming to church. It instilled within me an urgency to get my life in order: to prepare *temporally* for the upheavals of the latter days, and to be *spiritually* ready for the Second Coming of Christ. A little Refiner's fire directed at me is probably a blessing. I need that divine purifying and sanctifying which I can't attain any other way.

Some of the righteous may be caught in the *crossfire* directed at the wicked during the final sweep of God's wrath across the earth. "For, behold, the day cometh, that shall burn as an oven; and all the proud, yea, and all that do wickedly, shall be stubble; and the day that cometh shall burn them up, saith the Lord of hosts, that it shall leave them neither root nor branch" (Malachi 4:1). My view as a child of *stubble* was my dad's scratchy whiskers when he'd kiss me on days he didn't shave. It really wasn't so bad. Later as a teenager on a family trip to visit LDS Church history sites, I saw acre after acre of corn stalks growing skyward. Where the ground was left to fallow, useless stubble remained in the fields. I saw how barren the landscaped looked in contrast to the endless green rows of corn. Then I could better imagine the earth—and and the proud and wicked—being burned to stubble by the Refiner's fire.

Yet Jesus assures us that He has power to heal those who have faith in Him: "But unto you that fear my name shall the [Son] of righteousness arise with healing in his wings" (Malachi 4:2).

Develop Soul Power

When we rely on Jesus Christ to heal us in times of trial, we develop soul power. Even in midst of the Refiner's fire, our faith can override fear and give us strength. I'm reminded of Giant Sequoia trees that can withstand forest fires to remain some of the oldest living organisms on earth. Many of their trunks show charred scars forty or fifty feet upward. Sequoias produce tannin which repels fire and which was formerly used in the treatment of humans' burns. The bark around a Sequoia's trunk can be as thick as two feet. After a fire, it develops an even hardier bark to heal and conceal the wound so the tree can live endless years onward.

In a similar way, Christ's Atonement covers our scars and heals our wounds so we can extend our lives into eternity. "He healeth the broken in heart, and bindeth up their wounds" (Psalm 147:3). It's up to us, however, to turn unto Him and repent of our errors in order to receive His incomparable mercy. If our gaze is continually focused on Christ, we will be blessed, according to our faith.

> The greatest tragedy of life is that, having paid that awful price of suffering 'according to the flesh that his bowels might be filled with compassion' and now prepared to reach down and help us, [the Savior] is forbidden because we won't let him. We look down instead of up. [Truman G. Madsen "Prayer and the Prophet Joseph," *Ensign*, January, 1976, p. 18]

How much better to look upward—open our minds to sublime knowledge and our hearts to His miraculous healing. As I learned on my spring walk amid the crackling pinecones, it can take more than one upward glance to comprehend all the lessons God offers. Like the people in the Nephite lands, we must repeatedly open our eyes and ears: "And again the *third time* they did hear the voice, and did open their ears to hear it; and their eyes were towards the sound thereof; and they did look steadfastly towards heaven, from whence the sound came.

"And behold, the *third time* they did understand the voice which they heard" (3 Nephi 11:5-6, italics added).

Hopefully, it won't take more than a third time for us to focus on Christ when He returns to earth. How precious to see Him clearly and hear Him speaking. He promised that the righteous "will hear my voice, and shall see me, and shall not be asleep, and shall abide the day of my coming; for they shall be purified, even as I am pure" (D&C 35:21).

When we allow the Refiner's fire to incinerate our sins, we offer God our sacrifice of a broken heart and contrite spirit. Elder Neal A. Maxwell said, "Real, personal sacrifice never was placing an animal on the altar. Instead, it is a willingness to put the animal in us upon the altar and letting it be consumed! Such is "the sacrifice unto the Lord ... of a broken heart and a contrite spirit" (D&C 59:8). ("Deny Yourselves of All Ungodliness," *Ensign,* 1995, 68).

Conclusion

Though the Refiner's fire might be harshly humiliating, it can also be a boost toward spiritual maturity. I say, bring it on! Maybe I'll roast hot dogs and marshmallows and make s'mores to share with others enduring the blaze. Of course, it's not until the flames fade to warm embers that any productive cooking can be done. At any rate, it's best to prepare in advance to survive the prophesied upheavals in the Last Days. Remember our Father chastens His children because of His love and desire for us to live eternally in the celestial kingdom. "For all those who will not endure chastening, but deny me, cannot be sanctified" (D&C 101:5).

Adversity has often companioned both ancient and modern-day leaders of Christ's Church. President Spencer W. Kimball patiently endured more than average afflictions during his life. He wrote the following to encourage others:

> Being human, we would expel from our lives physical pain and mental anguish and assure ourselves of continual ease and comfort, but if we were to close the doors upon sorrow and distress, we might be excluding our greatest friends and benefactors. Suffering can make saints of people as they learn patience, long-suffering, and self-mastery. [*Faith Precedes the Miracle*, 98]

Becoming saints is a lengthy struggle for most of us, but our Exemplar Jesus Christ admonished, "Be ye therefore perfect" (Matthew 5:48). Without doubt, He meant what He said. We are required to complete the entire process of sanctification before we can dwell in God's presence. Even if it's painful, even if we get singed with the Refiner's fire, we are in for the full treatment. Only by purging our sins and purifying our souls can we achieve perfection through the grace of Christ's Atonement. Never despair in the midst of fiery trials, for Jesus Christ will comfort and encourage us each step of the way:

> *When through fiery trials thy pathway shall lie,*
> *My grace, all sufficient, shall be thy supply.*
> *The flame shall not hurt thee; I only design*
> *Thy dross to consume and thy gold to refine.*
> ["How Firm a Foundation," *Hymns*, no. 85]

For additional insight see the following:

- Neal A Maxwell, "Deny Yourselves of All Ungodliness," *Ensign*, May 1995, 66–68
- Howard W. Hunter, "God Will Have a Tried People," *Ensign*, May 1980, 24–26.
- Richard G. Scott, "Peace of Conscience and Peace of Mind," *Ensign*, Nov. 2004, 15–18.

For God so loved the world,
that he gave his only begotten Son,
that whosoever believeth in him, should not perish,
but have everlasting life.
John 16:3

God So Loved the World

Where would we be without the incomprehensible love of our Heavenly Father, who sent His Beloved Son to redeem us? I stand all amazed that "God so loved the world, that he gave his only begotten son, that whosoever believeth in him should not perish, but have everlasting life" (John 3:16). Miraculous and unequaled, Christ's Atonement is something none of us can live without—in this world as well as the next life. "Herein is love, not that we loved God, but that he loved us, and sent his Son to be the propitiation for our sins" (1 John 4:10).

After raising four children, I consider our Father's giving His Son as inconceivable. I had difficulty letting my children have the car keys, for fear they would die in an accident. How could our Father bear to watch His Beloved Son be brutally nailed upon a cross? It must have been excruciating for our Father when Jesus "was wounded for our transgressions, he was bruised for our iniquities: the chastisement of our peace was upon him; and with his stripes we are healed." Certainly, "All we, like sheep have gone astray; we have turned every one to his own way; and the Lord hath laid on him the iniquity of us all" (Isaiah 53:5-6).

Jesus was the Master Healer. He cured the sick, blind, deaf, and lame. He also cast out devils, restored mental health, and raised the dead. Yet His greatest mending miracles, then and now, are healing disheartened souls. The phrase "with his stripes we are healed" will thunder through all eternity.

Then why so somber? Is that necessary? Reverential, yes. But somber, no. We ought to light sparklers, set off fireworks, and celebrate such divine intervention. We should cheer and shout to the world about the redemptive power of God's love. Like Alma, we might desire to "go forth and speak with the trump of God, with a voice to shake the earth" (Alma 29:1). However, we may find it difficult to explain the sublime and extraordinary pure love of Christ in ordinary human vocabulary.

Heavenly Father and Jesus love us in a supreme way—perhaps in a manner we cannot fully fathom. It's love that heals and comforts, while at the same time it purges our impurities to sanctify and redeem us.

Spiritual Redemption

Please bear with me as I share a personal experience when I pled with God to restore my spiritual health. At the time it occurred, my grief and anguish were tremendous, and to again bring it all to mind sorrows me. Yet I hope this account will benefit others, and I pray you will read it with patience and spiritual understanding.

There was a time when I committed a sin grievous enough to warrant a serious visit to my bishop. That may shock you. But not as much as it shocked me. I had done something dreadfully wrong—not a mere repent-at-the-bedside sin. I wondered if I could bear the humiliation and shame of admitting my mistake to my bishop. Yet I felt confessing would be far better than carrying such a cumbersome sin. I could not imagine what would happen if my family, friends, and ward members found out I'd been a bad girl. And I feared for the worst: that I would be excommunicated.

The most common types of LDS Church discipline are excommunication, disfellowship, and probation. Excommunication is the most severe. The person loses his priesthood, if he has been ordained, and he or she loses temple endowments and sealings. It is as if the person never received baptism or the gift of the Holy Ghost. A man is not permitted to attend priesthood meetings, but a man or woman may attend other meetings. However, an excommunicated person may not participate in discussions, say prayers, speak in church, nor partake of the sacrament.

Disfellowshipping may seem less severe, for the covenants in the temple are not broken, the priesthood is not removed, and the Holy Ghost does not withdraw. The person is not permitted to speak or pray in church, partake of the sacrament, nor have a temple recommend.

Probation, formal or informal, is prescribed by a bishop, branch president, or higher leader, who lays out a specific program for the person to follow.

When I succumbed to temptation, I feared I would die in a car crash or some other tragedy would befall me before I could fully repent. As soon as I returned home, I called my bishop and made the earliest possible appointment. Believe me, it was no picnic to go and confess what I had done. I would have rather sat down in a den of irate porcupines. Not that my bishop was irate or prickly. He was merciful, as I believe my Savior would have been. He did not excommunicate or disfellowship me. He put me on formal probation with a list of seven requirements to follow. Two items seemed especially harsh: For six months, he took away my temple recommend, and he forbid me to partake of the sacrament. I was certain everyone in the ward would notice when week after week I had to pass the sacrament tray by, especially when I was sitting on the stand in the choir. I thought that my not attending ward or stake temple nights would also clue my neighbors into questioning my unworthiness.

Anyone could speculate about what sin I committed to warrant Church probation. But at this point, it no longer matters. We all make mistakes. "For all have sinned, and come short of the glory of God" (Romans 3:23). Some of us just make more horrendous errors than others. I needed to be humbled, to learn a critical lesson, and to discover first-hand the blessings of repentance.

Whether large or small, earth-shaking or minor, every sin severs us from God. How excruciating that can be, as Alma admitted, "I was thus racked with torment,… harrowed up by the memory of my many sins,… in the gall of bitterness, and … encircled about by the everlasting chains of death … there could be nothing so exquisite and so bitter as were my pains" (Alma 36:17-18, 21).

What's important is not the depth of our sin but the quality of our repentance. When we completely satisfy the laws of justice, we can be healed, made clean, become whole, and receive sanctification through the Savior's merciful Atonement. "Come now, and let us reason together, saith the Lord: Though your sins be as scarlet, they shall be as white as snow; though they be red like crimson, they shall be as wool" (Isaiah 1:18).

Some people believe LDS Church discipline is a form of punishment. But I can testify that it is an act of love—pure love from our Savior who willingly took our sins upon Himself.

During my time on probation, I cried buckets of tears. There were days I needed sandbags at my chin to keep the flood of tears from running over my jaw and spilling onto my clothes. I prayed, fasted, and pled mightily with Heavenly Father to forgive me and to heal my wounded spirit. Each Sunday I agonized when I could not partake of the sacrament. Whenever I drove past the Salt Lake Temple, I anguished over my unworthiness to go inside.

Had there been hidden cameras in my house, they'd have shown my many sleepless nights of trying to find peace and solace— endlessly studying scriptures for comfort. Yet I would shrink to read passages like Alma 45:16 "for the Lord cannot look upon sin with the least degree of allowance." Also 3 Nephi 9:2 "wo unto the inhabitants of the whole earth except they shall repent; for the devil laugheth, and his angels rejoice… because of their iniquity."

My predicament was no laughing matter to me. The truth was, my spiritual reservoir had gone dry, and I had attempted to refill it by using the philosophies of the world. What I really needed to assuage the drought in my soul was not a fountain of youth, but a fountain of spirituality. I needed that living water Jesus spoke about to the woman of Samaria, "But whosoever drinketh of the water that I shall give him shall never thirst; but the water that I shall give him shall be in him a well of water springing up into everlasting life" (John 4:14).

I have related my bitter experience not because it's something I'm proud of, but because the Spirit prompted me to do so. I want you to know that I speak from experience where repentance is concerned. Any burden of sin, even a tiny sin, is grievous. Carrying sin is punishment, while repentance is healing. I have experienced the tremendous blessing of joy that replaces the torment of sin. "And oh, what joy, and what marvelous light I did behold; yea, my soul was filled with joy ... there can be nothing so exquisite and sweet as was my joy" (Alma 36:20-21).

Blessings of Repentance

Although repentance is a simple principle, it is not easy to endure. It's vital to remember that blessings come "after the trial of your faith" (Ether 12:6). If I explained how much I ached, agonized, and anguished, you would toss this book in the trash for making you depressed. Therefore, I must also relate the blessings that followed. That doesn't mean anyone should sin to seek blessings. It's so much better to follow the narrow path of righteousness.

After confessing and forsaking my grave sin, I believe I was forgiven and healed. The Lord spoke peace to me, as He did to the woman who was nigh to being stoned for her sins, "Neither do I condemn thee: go, and sin no more" (John 8:11).

Sin no more. What a simple yet edifying command! If only it were possible. I recently saw a billboard that read, "Avoid Road Rage. Stay out of cars!" Likewise, I would add, "Avoid pain and sorrow. Stay out of Satan's clutches!" How I wish to be totally free from sin in my life! Yet I still make mistakes I must repent of—lately more sins of ommission than commission.

Wouldn't it be nice to be like the people during King Benjamin's reign? Together, they "all cried with one voice, saying: Yea, we believe all the words which thou hast spoken ... because of the Spirit of the Lord Omnipotent, which has wrought a mighty change in us, or in our hearts, that we have no more disposition to do evil, but to do good continually" (Mosiah 5:2).

No one profits temporally or spiritually by committing sin—though Satan would have us believe we can. However, those who do get snared by his trappings are blessed when they turn to Christ and His Atonement for relief.

Some of my friends who read this book prior to its publication questioned whether I should relate this negative incident from my past. But I believe it can be a teaching tool, especially if I tell of the blessings that resulted. During my six months of probation I read the entire quadruple set of scriptures, so my knowledge of the gospel increased. After my probation ended, I performed endowment sessions twice each week for several months at the temple. While there, I also could pray and worship in the celestial room and become closer to God.

Another phenomenon I can't fully explain is that many in my ward commented on my improved appearance. Some would boldly asked what I'd done—had a facial, lost weight, used more make up? I never quite knew how to respond. Several stopped my husband in the hallway at church to say, "Your wife has surely become beautiful." I suppose a few thought I'd had plastic surgery. Actually, it was more like spiritual surgery. The Lord opened my heart, cleansed my wounded soul, and mended my broken spirit. Perhaps that allowed the Light of Christ to shine in my countenance.

My bishop must have noticed, because he soon called me to teach the "spiritual living" lessons in Relief Society. A few months after that, I asked his permission to relate in a lesson my experience with repentance. Later, as a result of that lesson, the bishop said a few sisters in the ward had come to him with confessions. They could now become healed through the Christ's infinite Atonement.

Repentance Brings Us To Christ

As outlined in the scriptures, humble penitence renders many blessings: forgiveness, joy, light, humility, hope, love, charity, peace, knowledge, healing, and the visitation of the Holy Ghost. Repentance brings us to Christ, through His selfless sacrifice.

Years ago, a Relief Society teacher meant to write "atonement" on the board. But she forgot to cross the first "T," so it read "alonement." During my repentance, I learned a great deal about alonement. Despite kind counsel from my bishop and loving concern from friends and family, I felt alone and isolated while on probation. I thought no one could understand my pain, and I anguished all the more because I had brought it upon myself.

Then I remembered Christ in Gethsemane. Surely, He understood! How alone He must have felt as He took upon himself the sins and sorrows of all mankind. Is it any wonder that He asked Peter, James, and John to stay nearby and be watchful? He wanted their support to ease His pain-filled atoning moment. And yet, He had to do this phenomenal deed by Himself. After an unfair trial, Jesus carried not only His cross to Calvary but also the burdens of all humankind. Alone in His suffering, He cried out in agony on the cross, "My God, My God, why hast thou forsaken me?" (Matthew 27:46). The statement below by Elder Melvin J. Ballard provides a stunning view of that moment:

So [God] bowed his head, and hid in some part of his universe, his great heart almost breaking for the love that he had for his Son. Oh, in that moment when he might have saved his Son, I thank him and praise him that he did not fail us, for he had not only the love of his Son in mind, but he had love for us, and I rejoice that he did not interfere, and that his love for us made it possible for him to endure to look upon the sufferings of his Son and give him finally to us, our Savior and our Redeemer. Without him, without his sacrifice, we would have been buried in the earth, and there our bodies would have remained, and we would never have come glorified into his presence. And so this is what it cost, in part, for our Father in Heaven to give the gift of his Son unto men. ["Classic Discourses from the General Authorities: The Sacramental Covenant," *New Era*, 1976, 11]

Christ had to suffer by Himself in order to be glorified. Similarly, each man and woman must seek salvation through individual repentance and obedience. No one can do it for us, no matter how demanding the task may be. "Come unto the Lord with all your heart, and work out your own salvation with fear and trembling before him" (Mormon, 9:27).

Christ Carries Our Burdens

In January of 1985, my parents left to serve in the Singapore Mission, which then covered several Asian countries. When I took them to the airport, they had lots and lots of baggage—enough to last them for a year. What a struggle to unload it all from my car and convey it to the airline check-in counter. Awkward! Heavy! Like they'd packed a thousand iron rods, which is the word of God, right? (See 1 Nephi 15:23-24). When we piled all their luggage together for airline tags, the scale read 172 pounds! How grateful I was that we did not have to carry it further. What a relief to set it down and let someone else worry about it.

That is like the burden of sin. Hopefully, we'll only struggle to carry such baggage for a short time before we repent and give the weighty load to our Savior. The amazing part is that Jesus volunteered for this heavy-duty responsibility!

Christ's Atonement will have no affect on our forgiveness if we fail to fully repent. But if we have true intent to change and improve, we are blessed by *The Miracle of Forgiveness*, as President Spencer W. Kimball titled the book in which he wrote the following:

> To every forgiveness there is a condition. The plaster must be as wide as the sore. The fasting, the prayers, the humility must be equal to or greater than the sin. There must be a broken heart and a contrite spirit. There must be "sackcloth and ashes." There must be tears and genuine change of heart.... There must be restitution and a confirmed, determined change of pace, direction, and destination. [*The Miracle of Forgiveness*, 353]

Sometimes I wonder where I'd be without the Atonement. Though I am the one who has erred, in both big and small ways, Jesus Christ, who was sinless and perfect, sacrificed His life to save me. It seems more fair that it should have been my own hands and feet nailed upon the cross to suffer for my iniquities.

I've heard it said "Jesus came to pay a price He did not owe, because we owed a price we could not pay." I cannot reimburse the Savior with any amount of equity for His suffering and sacrifice. The only way to return His eternal grace is by giving up my natural self and placing my soul in His keeping. I must make Him the center of all I do and say, the sum of my existence, the very reason I live and breathe.

The more I can put my human nature aside and allow His divine influence to guide me, the more I can become like Him. No compromising is allowed. No holding back. I must bow down before Him whole-heartedly with pure faith. And then, through His profound mercy, He can make something better of me—vastly improved from anything I could manage on my own. It may take a long time and cost me huge amounts of humility and self-sacrifice, but it is the only way to overcome my human frailties and stretch toward godliness. Whatever the price, I am willing to pay with my entire life and with a fulness of love for Him, as He has offered all His life and love for you and me.

To love God with all your heart, soul, mind, and strength is all-consuming and all-encompassing. It is not a lukewarm endeavor but a total commitment of our entire being—physically, mentally, emotionally, and spiritually.

The enormity of God's love extends into every facet of our lives. All our thoughts and hopes, all our actions and deeds, whether spiritual or temporal, should be founded upon our love of the Lord. "Let all thy thoughts be directed unto the Lord ... forever" (Alma 37:36). President Ezra Taft Benson taught, "When we put God first, all other things fall into their proper place or drop out of our lives. Our love of the Lord will govern the claims of our affection, the demands on our time, the interests we pursue, and the order of our priorities." (*The Teachings of Ezra Taft Benson*, 350)

No matter what activities crowd your days, you can choose to focus on the things of eternal importance. Life is not about finding a hairdresser you like. Forget about keeping up with the Joneses or the Cannons and Smiths. I can't even keep pace with Bart Simpson's family. If you happen to get snared by the cares of the world, go take a cold shower and read the scriptures. And remember, if at first you don't succeed, you can either destroy all evidence that you tried, or you can "try, try again."

When all is said and done, I know that neither the Father or Son will be satisfied until I obtain absolute perfection. In the meantime, They will be happy with each faltering move I make toward losing myself and becoming one with Them. Though I might start by crawling, and my early steps may falter, the Lord will be there to encourage my faithful progress until I'm able to complete the straight and narrow pathway to life eternal.

Without God's intervention, I'm like a spongy jellyfish, bobbing uselessly in the ocean currents. But with God's assistance, I can do many things beyond my normal capabilities. I like the way C. S. Lewis illustrates this concept:

> What do we mean when we talk of God helping us? We mean God putting into us a bit of Himself, so to speak. He lends us a little of His reasoning powers and that is how we think: He puts a little of His love into us and that is how we love one another. When you teach a child writing, you hold its hand while it forms the letters: that is, it forms the letters because you are forming them. We love and reason because God loves and reasons and holds our hand while we do it. [*Mere Christianity*, 45]

The Love Of God

Vivid illustrations of God's pure love are provided in Lehi's dream of the tree of life. While partaking of the fruit, he found it far exceeded anything he'd ever eaten. Lehi described it as "desirable above all other fruit," "to make one happy," "most sweet, above all," and "white, to exceed all whiteness" (1 Nephi 8:10-12).

When Nephi yearned for greater understanding of the tree's meaning, he inquired of God. He then learned that the fruit exceeded "all beauty," and it represented "the love of God, which ... is the most desirable above all things." The angel also declared it as the "most joyous to the soul" (1 Nephi 11:8-9, 21-23).

Such desirable fruit would be a great improvement to home gardens and orchards. Wouldn't it be wonderful if the seeds were available to plant in the soil? Then we could await the emergence of a miraculously growing vine, like Jack's giant beanstalk, which could take us to the treasured land above. Of course, Jack's story was only a fairy tale. But Lehi's dream was prophetic. It can come true for those who keep eternal covenants. As Latter-day Saints, we believe in the literal opportunity to eat fruit from the glorious tree of life. The reward is worth striving toward, as Alma attests:

But if ye will nourish the word [of God], yea, nourish the tree as it beginneth to grow, by your faith with great diligence, and with patience, looking forward to the fruit thereof, it shall take root; and behold it shall be a tree springing up unto everlasting life.

And because of your diligence and your faith and your patience with the word in nourishing it, that it may take root in you, behold, by and by ye shall pluck the fruit thereof, which is *most precious*, which is *sweet above all* that is sweet, and which is *white above all* that is white, yea, and *pure above all* that is pure; and ye shall feast upon this fruit even until ye are filled, that ye hunger not, neither shall ye thirst.

Then, my brethren [and sisters], ye shall reap the rewards of your faith, and your diligence, and patience, and long-suffering, waiting for the tree to bring forth fruit unto you (Alma 32:41-43, italics added).

Indeed, the tree of life can spring "up unto everlasting life," if we individually nourish it with patience, faith and diligence. Partaking of the fruit, the pure love of God, should be our ultimate goal, since it's beyond anything on earth for which we might hope.

It ranks above all things as most sweet, most white, most beautiful, most joyous, most desirous, most precious, and most pure.

When Lehi discovered everlasting joy in the fruit of God's love, he longed for all his family to join him and partake of it. Righteous parents have similar desires. Most will do everything in their power to lead their children toward everlasting life.

Working Together with Faith

There are weeks, even months, when family life is as chaotic as a swap meet. That may be the reason that the first word babies often say is "Uh-oh!" If they have older siblings, it's usually "Ow!" I remember more than one day of motherhood that seemed a total waste of prayer power. A mother has to run on rechargeable batteries, with no bonus for working overtime. She can repair mysteriously-plugged toilets, leap over flaming trash cans in a single bound, and she is able to bite her tongue when talking to teenagers. Gratefully, my motherhood memories include more positive than negative experiences in raising four children. Most of the time we joyfully pulled together, such as the time Glenn and I took our children backpacking to Coyote Gulch. You may recall I had been lost in that area before. And I decided to take our children there? What was I thinking?

It's a long drive from Salt Lake City to the desert south of Escalante, Utah. Though we'd hoped to arrive earlier, it was sundown when we started on the trail. Wispy clouds glowed pink and orange while we hiked three miles through sandy soil and cactus. When finally we peered down into Coyote Gulch, everything was enveloped in twilight gray—the boulders around us, the stony canyon walls, the shallow stream far below, the clouds, the sky. The moon was only a thin crescent rising in the east.

For a moment we stood like statues, in awe of the desert landscape, while we tried to discern the best way to rappel down into the gulch. Staying atop the cliff was not the answer. Winds blow chill across the desert at night, and we had no tents. Down in the gulch, we could sleep beneath overhanging arches of stone, sheltering us from the wind and the possibility of rain. Also, our only source of water was from seeps in the cliff walls that fed the small river below.

I had descended this cliff twice before, and my husband had once, but we had done it only in daylight. Even with a rope secured at my waist, the rappeling had not been easy, especially while balancing a forty-pound pack on my back. As a mother, I worried about my four children making the descent in near darkness. Our sons, Colin and Quinn, age fourteen and eleven, were agile and fearless enough to view this as a grand adventure. But our youngest son Ryan, was only seven, and I hoped he could manage the cliff with the rest of us helping. My chief concern was for our daughter Erin, age twelve, who has had a chronic eye disease most of her life. Despite several surgeries to correct her vision, I knew she did not see well, especially in dark or shadowed locations.

Glenn and I decided initially to send our oldest son down the cliff. Colin had rappeled the 150-foot cliff once before, guided by a Boy Scout leader. That night with our family, he eagerly tied the rope around his waist and negotiated his way down the rocky terrain. He then left his backpack at the bottom of the cliff before pulling himself back to the rim. His adolescent muscles were needed to assist Glenn and Quinn in holding the rope for others to rappel into the gulch.

As denser darkness enveloped us, we pondered how best to get our visually impaired daughter down the cliff. Erin took off her backpack and left it at the top for Colin to bring down later. Then we decided to anchor the rope around both her and me. Though I had often used a bowline knot, I'd never tied it around two people together. After knotting the rope at my waist, I pulled Erin close against my chest and tied another bowline around her. Now it was a matter of faith for Erin and me to navigate this cliff together. Though my awkward pack tugged at my shoulders, I knew God could ease my burden, as He had lightened the burdens on the backs of Alma's people (see Mosiah 24:14–21).

With Glenn, Colin, and Quinn grasping the rope, I began to rappel the steep slope with my daughter. First I searched out a secure spot on the rocky face and placed my foot there. In the dim light, Erin could barely see my white shoe, but she was able to step down and wedge her foot against mine. Then I firmly fixed my second foot, and she placed her other one atop mine. And so it went, one careful step after another down the sheer incline.

I was unaware of the passage of time but keenly aware of my pounding heart and jittery nerves. Erin only once let out a cry of fear as she momentarily lost her balance. But she quickly stabilized with my arms around her and the rope held securely by her dad and brothers. With the family helping our courageous effort, Erin and I finally reached flat ground.

In our time of need, I'm certain the Lord was also watching over us. I thought of how we're advised to follow our Savior's footsteps, just as Erin followed mine in that precarious circumstance. Whenever darkness seems to envelop our lives, we might barely be able to see the way. But step after step Jesus Christ leads us toward eternal life.

That night, I untied the rope from me and Erin, then watched as it was pulled upward until the end disappeared in darkness. Then I found a flashlight in my backpack and shined it upward so our sons could more clearly find footholds on the craggy slope.

Ryan, the youngest and lightest, soon bounded down the cliff. Secured by the rope, he merely jumped from spot to spot in his descent until, with a big grin, he landed next to me and Erin. Quinn, our risk-taking child, then took his turn to tie on the rope. He, too, leaped downward in wide arcs to reach us. Finally Colin, hoisting Erin's backpack, lowered himself on the rope. He doffed his load alongside the other backpacks, and we had a group hug.

We remained huddled together while anxiously awaiting Glenn's descent. First he anchored one end of the rope around a huge boulder, then he knotted the other end at his waist. I grinned to see him stick a small flashlight in his teeth to add to the light I shined on the cliff. The five of us stood in suspense below while watching him ease his way down the jagged formation.

What an incredible sense of joy when our family all made it safely to our destination! Before long, we had unpacked our belongings, rolled out sleeping bags, and heated water for hot chocolate. Then we stretched out our sore muscles and relaxed our strained nerves. Not one of the kids complained about missing the TV or computer, though I knew by morning I might be longing for my cozy bed at home. As I lay quietly amid the buzz of mosquitoes and croak of frogs, my spirit reveled in how our family had pulled together with both faith and works to find joy together in this resting place.

That is how the gospel of Jesus Christ is meant to work. Together we exert faith and diligence to become worthy of resting in our heavenly home. Though some may have weaknesses and others strengths, with each individual doing his or her best, a family or ward or similar group can assist each other to reach the goal of exaltation.

Conclusion

Of course, it all sounds good on paper. Often it's easier to read about the principles of the gospel than to live them. But God is pleased when we make righteous choices. Picture Him smiling down from heaven and giving us a "thumbs-up" signal. He truly is concerned that we become the individuals He intends us to be. He devotes all His attention toward our salvation and gives us all of His love. In return, He would like us to give Him not just a portion of our energy and time and talents, but all our love and devotion.

Our Father's love is so powerful, so encompassing that His arms are forever outstretched, beckoning us to come unto Him and partake of all He has to offer. Whether or not we recognize it, His love has sustained us, not just in our earthly lives, but long before our mortal births.

There is in all of us an apparently infinite, and certainly ultimate, need for a rich, abiding, undergirding, trustworthy love. This is a love that reaches in and through the self, outward to others, and upward to the highest in the universe. In the ordinary world, even the world of religion, this craving finds extremely rare fulfillment, though it is talked sbout ceaselessly.... man was known and loved profoundly even prior to mortal birth; that love, indeed, drew him and his Eternal Father together in a sphere of perfected light and glory. [Truman G. Madsen, *Eternal Man*, 8-9].

God's intense love may be hard to define in words. Those who have felt it might say as Nephi, "He hath filled me with his love, even unto the consuming of my flesh" (2 Nephi 4:21).

Though celestial, eternal love from the Father and Son is comforting, healing, and soothing, at the same time it can pierce our souls to refine, purify, and sanctify us. We may have difficulty enduring such intense love, and perhaps we are not quite prepared to accept its profundity. But it is always at hand for us to receive.

What unfathomable love we receive from our Father in Heaven, who allowed His Son to be cruelly crucified. What selfless love Jesus exudes that He would bleed from every pore, and suffer Himself to be nailed upon a cross. Perhaps it was not the nails that kept Him fastened there, but His pure love for us. Those who take firm hold on God's pure love will understand Paul's declaration:

> If God be for us, who can be against us?...
> Who shall separate us from the love of Christ? shall tribulation, or distress, or persecution, or famine, or nakedness, or peril, or sword?...
> Nay, in all these things we are more than conquerors through him that loved us.
> For I am persuaded, that neither death, nor life, nor angels, nor principalities, nor powers, nor things present, nor things to come,
> Nor height, nor depth, nor any other creature, shall be able to separate us from the love of God, which is in Christ Jesus our Lord. [Romans 8:31, 35, 37-39]

For additional insight see the following:

- Russell M. Nelson, "Divine Love," *Ensign*, February 2003, 20-25.
- 1 John, chapters 3 and 4
- Spencer W. Kimball, *The Miracle of Forgiveness*, Salt Lake City, Bookcraft, 1969.

Beloved, if God so loved us,
we ought also to love one another.
1 John 4:11

Love One  Another

Because the Father's and Son's love is infinite, shouldn't we endeavor to share Their generous love with others? It's not always easy to do. We may feel like the teenaged boy who asked in Sunday School, "How can God love all the people in the world? I can't manage just the five in our family."

While Jesus stood amidst a group of people, one of the scribes asked Him a simple question, "Which is the first commandment of all?" (Mark 12:28). Without hesitation Jesus provided this potent reply:

> The first of all the commandments is, Hear, O Israel; The Lord our God is one Lord:
> And thou shalt love the Lord thy God with all thy heart, and with all thy soul, and with all thy mind, and with all thy strength: this is the first commandment.
> And the second is like, namely this, Thou shalt love thy neighbour as thyself. There is none other commandment greater than these. [Mark 12:29-31]

It seems strange that we must be *commanded* to love God, who is the Father of our spirits. Our love for Him should be as natural as love for an earthly father. Since we look to Jesus Christ for redemption from sin and death, it should be easy to love Him, too. I've heard it said, "God sent Jesus to earth as love, so we could learn to love as Jesus."

Unfortunately, we are somewhat flawed as human beings. I hope it doesn't deflate your ego to realize that. I'm not simply talking about physical defects that might require coronary bypass surgery or radiation treatment.

Our spirits are only partially developed and need strengthening. Some of us, thanks to Satan's discouraging tactics, may think we're beyond help. When our imperfections keep our spirits from performing at peak levels, then our giving love can seem half-hearted. What if Christ's Atonement had been half-hearted? What if He had given only 50% or 80%? Which of us would not be saved?

Look On The Heart

I like to think that God's pure love is reciprocal—that because He loves us, we should love Him and love all His children. John, who was called "beloved" by Jesus, in turn called other people beloved. This is especially evident in his epsitles, wherein he wrote, "Beloved, if God so loved us, we ought also to love one another" (1 John 4:11).

During my adolescent years, I learned a phrase that is as true now as it was then: "There are two types of people in the world: those you love, and those you don't know." Because we fail to take time to know and understand strangers, we may miss the opportunity to learn to love them. We tend to peer at life through skeptical rather than spiritual eyes, and often we judge others according to their appearance.

A friend of mine had stopped her car for a traffic signal at a busy intersection. While waiting for the red light to switch to green, she enjoyed the spring breeze blowing through the open window. Then from a corner of her eye, she caught sight of a man crossing the street. His T-shirt was grimy, and he wore tattered trousers and run-down shoes. He came with a haphazard step, as if he'd imbibed too much liquor.

As the ragged man neared my friend's car, rather than continuing across the pedestrian lane, he veered directly toward her car window. "Oh, great!" she mumbled to herself while tightening her grip on the steering wheel. "He's coming to ask me for money. Then he'll waste it on more alcohol." With no time to roll the window shut, all she could do was look aside and pretend to adjust the radio.

In the next instant, the man's raspy voice boomed, "Good morning, M'am!" She turned to find herself face-to-face with his missing-teeth smile. Though she scowled back at him, he continued in a cheery voice, "You have a nice day, okay?" Then he jauntily walked back to the pedestrian lane and finished crossing the street.

Though my friend expected a negative encounter, the man offered her kind words and a smile. Though his clothes were grimy and tattered, his heart was pure at that moment.

How quickly we are to judge what we see on the outside while overlooking the goodness inside others. Remember God's direction to the Prophet Samuel, who sought a new king for Israel. "But the Lord said unto Samuel, Look not on his countenance, or on the height of his stature,... for the Lord seeth not as a man seeth; for man looketh on the outward appearance, but the Lord looketh on the heart" (1 Samuel 16:7).

Perhaps it's difficult to "love thy neighbor as thyself" because we fail to love ourselves. We might put ourselves down for the simplest things, such as eating chocolate, which actually isn't mentioned in the Word of Wisdom. Others may chide themselves for gossiping for hours on the phone, yet they are unable to think of anything to say when they pray. How easy for the devil to dissuade us in feeling good about ourselves, even with our knowledge that we are children of God. One of Satan's prime schemes is to make us depressed about sins for which we've already repented. But God said, "I, the Lord, will forgive whom I will forgive, but of you it is

required to forgive all men" (D&C 64:10). I believe God meant what
He said. We are required to forgive everyone, *including ourselves.*

The Least Of These

Those who seem to be the hardest to love are the ones who
actually need it most. Isn't it in the midst of our own anguish and
suffering when we desire an outpouring of love? Whether or not
we deserve it at those times, doesn't our Heavenly Father often
send extra love our way? Even if we purposely distance ourselves
from Him, the Lord wants us to return to His safe sheepfold.
Parables about the lost sheep (Matt. 18:12-14) and the prodigal
son (Luke 15:11-32) remind us that every individual is important.

Perhaps you've read the popular story about footprints in the
sand. It implies that sometimes there are two pairs of footprints,
when Jesus is walking beside us. At other times we see only
one set of footprints, when He carries us through our trials. It's
wonderfully symbolic to think when times are tough that our
Savior lifts us in His arms throughout our hardships. But in truth,
we are constantly and continually carried by the Lord—whether
we realize it or not—from before our birth until our hair is white as
hoary frost. Isaiah wrote many edifying messages, some of which
are difficult to understand. But I believe the following verses are
clear:

> Hearken unto me, O house of Jacob, and all the remnant of the
> house of Israel, which are borne by me from the belly, which
> are carried from the womb;
> And even to your old age I am he; and even to hoar hairs will
> I carry you: I have made, and I will bear; even I will carry, and
> will deliver you. [Isaiah 46:3-4]

Perhaps the strongest plea for us to love all people, was in
Christ's portrayal of himself in place of the needy.

> For I was an hungred, and ye gave me meat. I was thirsty, and
> ye gave me drink. I was a stranger, and ye took me in.

Naked, and ye clothed me: I was sick, and ye visited me: I was in prison, and ye came unto me....

Verily I say unto you, Inasmuch as ye have done it unto one of the least of these my brethren, ye have done it unto me. [Matthew 25:35-36, 40]

As already stated, Jesus called the Apostle John "beloved." How would you feel to hear the Lord refer to you in that way? Perhaps, like me, you occasionally describe yourself as lazy, envious, or arrogant. Maybe you still think of yourself in terms of that nickname your dad called you when you wore diapers. How much better we'd be if we could earn the label *beloved*. Remember Christ's words at the Last Supper, "love one another; as I have loved you" (John 13:34).

In an effort to develop Christlike attributes, our learning to love one another as He has loved us should be paramount. Giving up our comfort zones is merely part of reaching out to others with the pure love of Christ. Jesus willingly gave up His entire life. His example and words teach us the ultimate gift of pure love: "Greater love hath no man than this, that a man lay down his life for his friends. Ye are my friends, if ye do whatsoever I command you" (John 15:9, 12-13).

How stunning! Jesus considers us His friends if we do as He commands. That doesn't mean, however, that we can only be friends with those who do the things we ask of them. On the contrary: We should give our love, time, energy, and service to all within our sphere of influence. And we should have no expectations of receiving anything in return. In an article addressed to children at Christmas time, President Spencer W. Kimball and his counselors provided this insight about unselfish and unconditional love:

Christmas is a glorious time of friendliness, unselfish giving, and love....

But sometimes our gift-giving becomes only an exchange, gifts given for gifts expected.

Never did the Savior give in expectation of receiving. He did not give shoes or toys or perfume or games or clothes. His gifts were precious and rare ones. He gave eyes to the blind, ears to the deaf, legs to the lame. He gave light in place of darkness, forgiveness to the repentant, and hope to the despairing. ["A Joy-filled Christmas to All the Children of the World from the First Presidency," *Friend*, Dec. 1980, 3]

Serve with Inspired Love

Somewhere I heard this phrase, "You can give without loving, but you cannot love without giving." Surely the Lord will inspire us to serve with love, if we always remember Him. At times when I have blessed the lives of others, I recognize it's because of Christ's pure love emanating through me. When such miracles occur, they leave me both electrified and humbled.

During the time my husband attended graduate school, we were parents of one child with a second on the way. Our ward leaders assigned us to be home and visiting teachers for a new family. For the sake of anonymity, I'll call them the Harmony family, though their life was far from harmonious.

We had little money ourselves, but this family was truly in need. Both the parents were mentally impaired, which meant it took longer for them to navigate through simple matters. They struggled with parenting their 3-year-old daughter. Paying for food, housing, and medical expenses seemed a constant stress.

The husband rarely kept a job for more than a few months, because of his mental disability. Through LDS Church employment, my husband helped him get a janitorial job at LDS Hospital. But Brother Harmony went inconsistently to work, so their family's lifestyle remained downtrodden.

The wife seemed clueless about housework. I've sometimes excused my own poor housekeeping by showing visitors a plaque in my kitchen: "Housework never killed anyone, but why take a chance?" Though I could assist Sister Harmony in washing soiled clothes and dishes, I was unable to help with bigger tasks because I was pregnant and had my own one-year-old in tow.

I noticed that Sister Harmony wore only two dresses, which she alternated for Sunday meetings, as well as Relief Society and Primary meetings—still held mid-weekly in the 1970s. Both dresses looked old and colorless. One day as I searched for fabric to make myself a new maternity dress, I felt inspired to make a dress for Sister Harmony. However, I was unsure of what size pattern to get, because she was rather heavy-set. Finally I guessed at a size, then purchased fabric and notions according to the instructions.

After cutting out the fabric, I had enough remaining pieces to make a matching dress for her three-year-old daughter. When the mother-daughter dresses were finally sewn, I wrapped them in pretty packages. Then one Tuesday afternoon, when I knew Sister Harmony would be serving in our ward library to prepare for Primary, I anonymously left the gifts on her doorstep.

The next day before Relief Society started, I watched this sister flit around the room asking several women if they'd left the dresses at her door. Sitting quietly on the back row, I witnessed her joy over the unexpected gifts. To avoid suspicion, I had to duck behind my son on my lap and hide my own delight. I overheard her say to the Relief Society president, "I just want to thank whoever it was. Do you know who did it?" The president, of course, had no idea who'd left the dresses. Throughout the meeting I avoided eye contact with Sister Harmony, then afterward I hurried home before my secret could be divulged.

On Sunday, Sister Harmony and her daughter rushed into the chapel during the opening hymn for Sunday School. How glad I was to see they wore the matching dresses! When they passed my row, I reached out to catch her arm and compliment her on the new outfits. Then I innocently said, "Oh, you both look so nice! Where did you get the dresses?" She smiled and said she'd have to tell me later.

As the mother and daughter took their seats three rows ahead of me, I marveled at how perfectly the dresses fit. It looked as if I'd measured both their figures and made the patterns to suit them precisely. Smiling in satisfaction, I sensed a warm inner glow. I knew it was due not to luck, but to inspiration from the Spirit, that I had sewn those dresses so well.

At the time my husband and I assisted the Harmony family, our money was tight, and what we provided them came from our meager budget. However, it was not a sacrifice, but a blessing to serve them. I learned that home and visiting teaching is not about ignoring the cobwebs and dirty dishes. Nor is it giving the lesson then saying, "Let us know if there's anything we can do for you." Rather, it means taking care of the Lord's sheep—as families or individuals.

Simple Miracles

Blessing a neighbor's life with love rarely requires more than a small investment of time or money. A simple note tucked under a door or a single flower plucked from your own garden may be all it takes to replace someone's frown with a smile. Mother Teresa wisely said, "We can accomplish something extraordinary by doing something ordinary with love … just one day at a time.… Intense love does not measure—it just gives" (Mother Teresa, *No Greater Love*, 31).

Jesus Christ freely offered miraculous deeds, one day at a time, to demonstrate pure love. His gifts of compassion were not measured out in small doses, nor did He only serve His closest friends. Whenever I'm inspired to perform acts of charity, they seem like miracles in the midst of ordinary life. In my efforts to emulate Christ's divine miracles, I keep in mind the following:

- Faith must be present before a miracle can occur.
- Compassion and mercy are shown throughout each miracle.
- Miracles cannot be performed to serve selfish purposes.
- Christ's miracles did not seem to be planned, but rather, they arose out of the situation at hand.
- Jesus concerned Himself first with spiritual matters, then with the temporal. When healing the man with palsy, Jesus first said, "Thy sins are forgiven thee," and then said, "Arise, and take up thy couch" (Luke 5:18-26).

- Miracles have a high moral goal. They further the purposes of the Father.

It's taken me more years than it should have to learn that the power of Christ's love flowing through me can produce miracles in others' lives. Many times I've been too busy trying to be the pilot rather than moving into the co-pilot's seat. Only God can enlarge my small gifts of love into something supernal. I must be myself, but forget myself and lose myself in His service—one simple act at a time.

Epistles in 1 John, chapters 3 and 4 provide good insight about the pure love of Christ, as in this verse: "If we love one another, God dwelleth in us, and his love is perfect in us.... There is no fear in love; but perfect love casteth out fear" (1 John 4:12, 18).

How remarkable! Love and fear are incompatible. Still, I sometimes find myself holding back, afraid to love in its pure and perfect form. Yet if God's love dwells within me, what reason do I have to fear? Paul, writing to Timothy, said, "For God has not given us the spirit of fear; but of power, and of love, and of a sound mind" (2 Timothy. 1:7).

Indeed, God has instilled us with love and power and the intelligence to use them constructively. It should not take a commandment to prompt our love. To put it simply, we should love just because we can.

Love Is Motivation

I remember when several women in our neighborhood went to help a family pack boxes before they moved. Though her husband, a physician, was at his office that day, their six children pitched in to labor hour after hour. One of the women who worked alongside two of the teenagers later commented on how obedient the kids had been. Their mother said with a smile, "I believe we are here on earth to learn to be obedient. So I make sure my children obey."

Her statement seemed to ring true. It meshed with a question I heard a Sunday School teacher ask, "What is the first law of heaven?" The class's immediate response was "obedience."

Yet after pondering this principle, I no longer think obedience is the first law of heaven. I believe what Jesus said: the first commandment is to love God with all my heart, and the second to love my neighbor as myself. Therefore, I am here on earth to learn how to love. That does not mean obedience to God is unimportant. But obedience alone seems rather empty. I prefer thinking I should love God so much that I yearn to be obedient. I obey Him out of love, not out of duty.

Much of the world's distress and suffering is caused by an absence of love—failure to love ourselves, to love God, to love our family, to love our neighbors, and so on. Lack of love causes pain, heartache, sorrow, and depression. It can lead to poor health and even suicide. In a global sense, our inability to love causes pride, animosity, conflict, and war. William Gladstone said, "We look forward to the time when the power of love will replace the love of power" (from Thomas S. Monson, *Ensign*, May 1994, 60).

When I forget to look with love on the heart of a neighbor, it's easy to say something I later regret. How much better to emulate the unfailing love of God and keep my lips closed, as I read once on a t-shirt, "Dear Lord, please keep your arm around my shoulder, and your hand over my mouth."

Love Is Power

Those experienced with pure love realize how powerful it is. Love prompts service. Love kindles kindness. Love inspires hope. Love heals wounded hearts and souls. Love changes lives. Think how wonderful it would be if everyone lived by these words:

There is no difficulty that enough love will not conquer; no disease that enough love will not heal; no door that enough love will not open; no gulf that enough love will not bridge; no wall that enough love will not throw down; no sin that enough love will not redeem.

It makes no difference how deeply seated may be the trouble, how hopeless the outlook, how muddled the tangle, how great the mistake; a sufficient realization of love will dissolve it all.

If only you could love enough, you would be the happiest and most powerful being in the world. [Emmet Fox, in one of his "Sparks of Truth" publications, now out of print]

Love, indeed, is power—a gentle power that provides peace, strength, and healing. In the Lord's prayer, Jesus said to our Father, "For thine is the *kingdom* and the *power*, and the *glory* for ever" (Matthew 6:13, italics added). The *kingdom* of God is a celestial realm, and "the *glory* of God is intelligence" (D&C 93:36, italics added). I believe the greatest *power* of God is love.

How vital it is to become like God and love in His pure and perfect manner. These words of Joseph Smith tell how vital it is to know and become like God:

Here, then, is eternal life—to know the only wise and true God; and you have got to learn how to be gods yourselves,... the same as all gods have done before you, namely, by going from one small degree to another, and from a small capacity to a great one; from grace to grace, from exaltation to exaltation, until you attain to the resurrection of the dead, and are able to dwell in everlasting burnings, and to sit in glory, as do those who sit enthroned in everlasting power.... They shall rise again to dwell in everlasting burnings in immortal glory. [*History of the Church*, 6:306]

Twice Joseph Smith repeated the phrase "dwell in everlasting burnings." I used to think such words applied to the wicked, suffering through hell and damnation in unquenchable fire. But in the paragraph above, the "everlasting burnings" apply to righteous individuals.

Undoubtedly, the celestial kingdom is permeated with inexpressible love. Those who feel worthy to abide God's all-encompassing mercy will feel comfortable in a celestial flame of love. Those who feel less worthy and cannot endure such vivid love will choose a lesser kingdom where they might be at ease. To those who have lived wicked and unrepentant lives, an intensity of love in their evil state would seem like unquenchable torment. Each of God's children has the agency to choose whether to be warmed in the fire of celestial love or to be exiled to the chill of outer darkness.

How vital it is for us to live in worthiness—not in absolute perfection while on this earth, but with dedicated intent, centered in Christ. Only the righteous will be able to survive and thrive in a saturation of celestial love. Only the worthy will be allowed to "dwell in everlasting burnings" and "sit in glory."

Conclusion

The concept of everlasting burnings of celestial love might be hard to comprehend. There is much about our future life with Heavenly Father and Jesus Christ that we do not fathom. Yet we don't have to totally understand pure love to utilize it in creating small miracles of kindness. Though we're mortal with human limitations, when the love of God surges within us, we can readily bless others' lives. Some people may need medical care and prescriptions. Most need only love and time and selfless service.

Pure love is a rare quality. It is one of the few virtues that multiplies by dividing. It will take immense faith and frequent practice to provide pure love in the way God does. During the passage of time and eternity, I hope all God's children can partake of His omnipotent love and exclaim as Lehi did, "I am encircled about eternally in the arms of his love" (2 Nephi 1:15).

For additional insight, see the following:

- Joseph B. Wirthlin, "Our Lord and Savior," *Ensign*, Nov. 1993, 7–10.
- 1 John, Chapters 3 and 4.
- Mother Teresa, *No Greater Love*, Novato, CA, 1997, New World Library.

And behold, I tell you these things that ye may learn wisdom;
that ye may learn that when ye are in
the service of your fellow beings
ye are only in the service of your God.
Mosiah 2:17

In the Service  of Your God

King Benjamin's speech is an event I wish I'd witnessed. He said, "Hearken unto me, and open your ears that ye may hear, and your hearts that ye may understand, and your minds that the mysteries of God may be unfolded to your view" (Mosiah 2:9).

The phrase "mysteries of God," fascinates me; but then, I suppose everyone enjoys a good mystery. King Benjamin went on to describe the manner by which he had served his people without thought of himself, for he was "only in the service of God" (Mosiah 2:16). Then he counseled them to serve with their whole souls.

> And behold, I tell you these things that ye may learn wisdom; that ye may learn that when ye are in the service of your fellow beings ye are only in the service of your God....
> I say unto you that if ye should serve him who has created you from the beginning, and is preserving you from day to day, by lending you breath, that ye may live and move and do according to your own will, and even supporting you from one moment to another—I say, if ye should serve him with all your whole souls yet ye would be unprofitable servants....

[Ye] are eternally indebted to your heavenly Father, to render to him all that you have and are (Mosiah 2:17, 21, 34).

Eternal indebtedness to God never dissipates. Though I may serve Him *all* my life with *all* my soul, I would still be an unprofitable servant. When, or perhaps if, I make it to heaven's gate, I'll probably be lined up behind Apostles, General Relief Society leaders, and others who've served to the nth degree. Then God might say, "Bonnie, what have you done during your time on earth?" It won't do to *pretend* I've been good, saying, "I flossed my teeth each night before saying my prayers." He already knows everything I've done or said. And thankfully, God won't compare me with others, but only with my own potential as His daughter.

By watching Christ's selfless service, the chief Apostle Peter gradually learned to serve. That didn't mean Peter was without weakness, for Jesus said to him, "Simon, Simon, behold, Satan hath desired to have you, that he may sift you as wheat.

"But I have prayed for thee, that thy faith fail not: and when thou art converted, strengthen thy brethren" (Luke 22:31-32).

Did you ever sense that Satan "hath desired to have you, that he may sift you as wheat"? Perhaps all of us have at different stages in our lives. If you feel like chaff before the whirlwind of Satan's powers, take heart. No doubt Jesus has also "prayed for thee, that thy faith fail not." What courage that gives us to become truly converted so we might strengthen others.

Conversion means consecration to the Lord. It "denotes changing one's views, in a conscious acceptance of the will of God (Acts 3:19). If followed by faith…, repentance, baptism,… and the reception of the Holy Ghost …, conversion will become complete, and will change a natural man into a sanctified,… purified person…. Complete conversion comes after many trials and much testing" (see "Conversion," Bible Dictionary).

Feed His Sheep

The last chapter of John relates a touching encounter between Peter and the resurrected Lord. Simon Peter went, with other disciples, to his former work as a fisherman. Perhaps he didn't yet realize what was expected of him after Christ's crucifixion. It doesn't mean he'd given up his faith and conversion to the Lord.

All night the disciples had toiled and caught no fish. At dawn, Jesus stood on the shore and asked "Children, have ye any meat? They answered him, No" (John 21:5). When He advised them to cast their net on the right side of the boat, it filled to overflowing. I like the symbolism of casting a net on the "right side," as if our labors are in vain unless we do it the right way, the Lord's way. When the disciples came ashore with a bursting net of fish, they found Jesus beside a fire of coals, cooking fish and bread. He invited them to share the meal, but "none of the disciples durst ask him, Who art thou? knowing that it was the Lord" (v. 12).

After dining, Jesus asked "Simon Peter,… lovest thou me more than these?" (v. 15). Peter said he did, and Jesus said, "Feed my lambs" (v.16). A second and third time the same words were exchanged. But "Peter was grieved because [Jesus] said unto him the third time, Lovest thou me? And he said unto him, Lord, thou knowest all things; thou knowest that I love thee. Jesus saith unto him, Feed my sheep" (v. 17).

What a tender expression of our Savior's love! "Feed my lambs. Feed my sheep." Surely He pleads that we do the same. Our own lives are blessed when we feed His sheep—daily, hourly, and minute by minute! As Elder Robert D. Hales said, "Conversion requires consecrating our lives to caring for and serving others who need … our gifts and talents. The Lord didn't say tend my sheep when it is convenient, watch my sheep when you aren't busy. He said feed my sheep and my lambs; help them survive this world, keep them close to you. Lead them to safety—the safety of righteous choices that will prepare them for eternal life" ("When Thou Art Converted, Strengthen Thy Brethren," *Ensign*, May 1997, 82).

Five Loaves and Two Fishes

One miraculous story from Christ's earthly ministry is His feeding a multitude of five thousand. It began with a simple offering from a boy with five barley loaves and two small fish.

After the multitude sat down on the grassy hillside, "Jesus took the loaves; and when he had given thanks, he distributed to the disciples, and the disciples to them that were set down; and likewise of the fishes as much as they would" (John 9:11) When the multitude were full and satisfied, Jesus asked his disciples to gather up anything that remained. "Therefore they gathered them together, and filled twelve baskets with the fragments of the five barley loaves, which remained over and above unto them that had eaten" (v. 13).

With a small gift from a boy, Jesus magnified the bread and fish to bless thousands of lives. This is true with most followers of Christ. Those who willingly give of themselves, in large or small ways, will find that the Lord multiplies their efforts. Elder James E. Faust expanded on this thought:

In our time, we seem to have forgotten the miracle of the five loaves and the two fishes in favor of the miracles wrought by the mind and hand of men. I refer to the marvels of modern transportation and the increasing sophistication of all scientific knowledge, including the new electronic highway....

We are also to understand and remember that we too, like the lad in the New Testament account, are the spirit children of our Heavenly Father, that Jesus is the Christ, our Savior, and the Redeemer of the world....

It has been said that this church does not necessarily attract great people but more often makes ordinary people great. Many nameless people with gifts equal only to five loaves and two small fishes magnify their callings and serve without attention or recognition, feeding literally thousands....

Any man or woman who enjoys the Master's touch is like potter's clay in his hands. More important than acquiring fame or fortune is being what God wants us to be. Before we came to this earth, we may have been fashioned to do some small good in this life that no one else can do.... If God has a work for those with many talents, I believe he also has an important work for those of us who have few. ["Five Loaves and Two Fishes," *Ensign*, May 1994, 5-6]

Enhanced by Christ's power, the service we give can be amplified to nourish thousands. At least that's the theory. But theories need demonstrations and tests to be proved. I know I need more practice in sharing my time, talents, and energy. I often ask myself why I'm reluctant to serve and give. Do I worry people will look at me as if I were a blue and yellow striped zebra? No. Often I'm simply lazy or exhausted. Sometimes I'm concerned that what I'm able to do will not be suitable for the situation.

Why is it that our human nature causes us to feel self-conscious when opportunities to serve arrive? Perhaps Satan has a hand in our feelings of vulnerability. If so, I wish he'd find something else to do with his hands—maybe knitting or crocheting.

In some instances, we can provide food, clothing, or shelter for those in need—we can offer our money and skills. But in every circumstance, the most universal gift we can offer is love. Also, we can share our faith and testimonies of Jesus Christ, so others might desire to come unto Him. Elder Jeffrey R. Holland's words remind us of Christ's example:

Jesus did not come to improve God's view of man nearly so much as He came to improve man's view of God and to plead with them to love their Heavenly Father as He has always and will always love them.... The love of God, the profound depth of His devotion to His children, they still did not fully know— until Christ came.

So feeding the hungry, healing the sick, rebuking hypocrisy, pleading for faith—this was Christ showing us the way of the Father, He who is "merciful and gracious, slow to anger, longsuffering and full of goodness" [*Lectures on Faith*, 1985, 42]. In His life and especially in His death, Christ was declaring, "This is *God's* compassion I am showing you, as well as that of my own." ["The Grandeur of God," *Ensign*, Nov. 2003, 72]

Show Compassion to Strangers

Every individual Jesus encountered was important to Him, whether Jew, Gentile, Samaritan, Roman, or Greek. In these latter days, it's still vital for all God's children to be included, until there are "no more strangers and foreigners, but fellow citizens with the saints, and of the household of God" (Eph. 2:19).

How can we bless others unless we get out of our comfort zones? We don't need FBI clearance to serve someone with whom we're not acquainted. Our only concern should be to practice going from zero to sixty in three seconds so we're ready to serve whenever and wherever we're needed.

Eleven years ago my husband and I moved into a new neighborhood. Though I tried to practice my "compassionate service cringe," my new Relief Society president ignored it. One day she phoned to ask me to go on an errand of mercy. She must have been desperate. I hardly knew anyone in this ward, but she asked me to reach out and serve.

"Sister Howell has gone into a coma," my Relief Society president said. "But her family feels she responds when people talk with her or read to her. I wondered if you could visit her in the next few days."

I was not acquainted with the Howells and mentioned that to the president. She said it didn't matter. "Okay," I agreed. "I can free up an hour tomorrow. I'll take my guitar and sing to her."

"That would be great. I'll let Brother Howell know you're coming."

Autumn leaves crunched as I strode to the unfamiliar front porch and rang the doorbell. Grasped in one hand, my guitar felt heavy, but it was nothing compared to the heavy sorrow on Brother Howell's elderly face. I introduced myself and explained why I had come. With a nod, he quietly led me upstairs to a bedroom shrouded in musty odors. I studied the knick-knacks and other remains of life cluttering the furniture and walls, while Brother Howell fetched a chair so I could sit at his wife's bedside. His mouth managed a half smile as I sat down and cradled my guitar. Then he excused himself to make a phone call.

I looked at this dear sister, tidily tucked under a sheet and blanket. Dying is not pleasant. Why would anyone want to believe in reincarnation—to live and die all over again? Parkinson's disease had shriveled Sister Howell into little more than skin and bones. Strands of thinning gray hair curled at her temples. Her eyes were slightly open in a comatose stare. I said to myself, "Well, this is futile. She isn't really there." Nevertheless, I flipped through pages of music, then began to sing.

Somewhere over the rainbow, way up high,
There's a land that I heard of once in a lullaby.
Somewhere over the rainbow, skies are blue,
And the dreams that you dare to dream really do come true.
["Over the Rainbow," words and music by E. Y. Harburg and Harold Arlen, 1938.]

Warmth flooded my soul. I sensed Sister Howell's dreams of soaring through celestial rainbows would soon come true. With my natural eyes, all I saw was her body, frail and decaying in that bed. But I knew her spirit was radiantly alive and prepared to be encircled eternally in God's love. A wistful sigh issued from my lips before I sang a series of popular tunes.

Though Sister Howell hovered between this life and the next, I believed she could hear my music. I hoped it was soothing and not grating on her nerves. The longer I sang, the more I believed she was not listening alone. I sensed the presence of supernal spirits in the room, and I yearned for the visual acuity to see them. Have you ever wished you could don camouflage clothes and disappear from a scene? That's how I felt. I wanted my physical body to vanish so the spirits would come into view. But that was not a miracle I could conjure up at the time.

In hopes of retaining the heavenly impression, I laid aside the popular music and opened a hymn book. Worldly matters faded from my mind as I strummed the sacred music. No longer did I smell the musty odor nor notice the clutter in the bedroom. Enveloped in a cocoon of serenity, I serenaded all who wished to listen to my untrained voice, including Brother Howell who had bravely come to stand beside the door.

Glancing up at him, I discerned his deep love for his wife. Beyond this human affection, I felt a celestial love permeate the room, as if our Heavenly Father was also nearby. Humbly, I expressed my emotions through song.

Where love is, there God is also.
And with Him we want to be.
Show us the way and guide us tenderly
That we may dwell with Him eternally.
["Where Love Is," *Children's Songbook*, 138-139]

Neither myself nor Brother Howell could keep from weeping. After a moment, he turned his face away and went downstairs. Through my tears, I shared more songs to soothe this precious daughter of God from earthly life into eternity.

It no longer mattered what other tasks awaited me on that calm autumn morning. I could not pull myself away. Communing with Sister Howell amid the intangible spirits lifted my soul. Though I'd planned to stay for less than an hour, hymn after hymn arose in my throat. I had initially come to fill a need for this family. Yet I was the one being filled. Nearly two hours passed. Gradually my voice weakened, and my hands wilted on the strings. I could only manage a few more songs, which I selected with care.

Jesus, the very thought of Thee,
With sweetness fills my breast.
But sweeter far thy face to see,
And in thy presence rest.
[*Hymns*, no. 141]

I somewhat envied Sister Howell for nearing the sacred moment of meeting the Lord. Would He speak her name? Would she tremble to behold the wounds in His feet, hands, and wrists? Would she weep to see how the sword had pierced His side?

Though I felt utterly unprepared to kneel before the Lord, I longed to be with Him. My voice quivered as I sang through "I Know That My Redeemer Lives." The third verse seemed especially poignant for this dying sister with shallow breath.

> *He lives and grants me daily breath.*
> *He lives, and I shall conquer death.*
> *He lives my mansion to prepare.*
> *He lives to bring me safely there.*
> [*Hymns*, no. 136]

I touched Sister Howell's hand—shriveled, cold, nearly lifeless—unlike her spirit that I knew was vibrant with energy. No longer did she seem like a stranger to me. We were sisters, daughters of God. Patting her frail flesh, I whispered, "You're going home. It will be glorious. You'll see the Savior. He's waiting to enfold you in His loving arms."

Overcome by my own celestial homesickness, I released Sister Howell's thin hand and searched for one last hymn. What I found had deep meaning for someone about to enter Christ's presence.

> *I need, thee, oh, I need Thee.*
> *Every hour I need Thee!*
> *Oh, bless me now, my Savior;*
> *I come to Thee!*
> [*Hymns*, no. 98]

Two days later, Sister Howell died. Though in the flesh she never spoke to me, my visit to her taught me much. By sharing my gifts with her, I also received a gift: a glimpse of the glorious peace beyond this earthly sphere.

Christ Provided A Pattern

During His ministry, Jesus provided a pattern for us to follow in our kind deeds to others. Those who don't serve their fellow men will not be flattened like asphalt by a steam roller. That's just a nasty rumor. However, they will miss valuable opportunities for blessings and growth.

One perfect example of Christ's selfless service was when He washed the feet of His disciples. Picture Him kneeling while His tender hands sponged off the grime and dirt from each man's feet. In some ways it was symbolic of what Jesus would do for all of us—that of kneeling in Gethsemane and cleansing away the filthy sins of the world through His Atonement.

After Jesus washed the disciples' feet, He offered a few words to remind them that no one, including Himself, was so superior as to not serve others.

> Ye call me Master and Lord: and ye say well; for so I am.
> If I then, your Lord and Master, have washed your feet; ye also ought to wash one another's feet.
> For I have given you an example, that ye should do as I have done to you.
> Verily, verily, I say unto you, The servant is not greater than his lord; neither he that is sent greater than he that sent him.
> If ye know these things, happy are ye if ye do them (John 13:4-6, 8-9, 12-14).

What a lovely portrayal of Christ's humility! He said we will be happy if we do as He has done. He also counseled His disciples in the Nephite lands, "Therefore, hold up your light that it may shine unto the world. Behold I am the light which ye shall hold up—that which ye have seen me do" (3 Nephi 18:24).

Watch One Hour

During His final hours, Jesus went to Gethsemane and took Peter, James, and John with Him. Though He often resorted to this garden for peace and meditation, that evening's prayer would not bring Him solace. Rather, He would be subject to the most excruciating torture in the history of earth. No wonder He wanted His three Apostles to be there and sustain Him through His agony. After asking them to tarry and watch with Him, "he went a little further, and fell on his face, and prayed, saying, O my Father, if it be possible, let this cup pass from me: nevertheless not as I will, but as thou wilt.

"And he cometh unto the disciples, and findeth them asleep, and saith unto Peter, What, could ye not watch with me one hour? (Matthew 26:38-40)

Despite the Lord's request for these three brethren to watch with Him, they went to sleep. I wonder if His words pierced their hearts with sorrow. I wonder, too, if I've been guilty of sleeping when the Lord has needed me. In like manner, He might say to me, "Bonnie, could ye not watch with me one hour?"

I hear an echo in my mind of that phrase in different forms: What, could you not go visiting teaching for one hour? Could you not serve a few hours in the temple? Could you not take a moment to pray? Could you not fast for twenty-four hours to bless the needy? Could you not serve extra time in your church calling? Could you not take time to read the scriptures? Could you not spare a few minutes to bear your testimony to a stranger?

It makes me squirm to recall times I should have served the Lord but didn't. I hope you are a more diligent child of God than I am. Perhaps you should be the one writing this book.

Conclusion

When we truly love the Lord, we won't hesitate to serve Him, as well as our "neighbors." When life is hectic, it seems easy to excuse ourselves by saying, "it is not requisite that a man should run faster than he has strength" (Mosiah 4:27). Perhaps a better verse to cite is, "I can do all things through Christ which strengtheneth me" (Philippians 4:13).

Only with faith in Jesus Christ can we do what is expedient. Without His limitless power, we can't fulfill the purposes for which we've been sent to earth. If at times we feel weak and unable to give, remember "that by small and simple things are great things brought to pass" (Alma 37:6). There is no blessing in being reluctant and no benefit in awaiting God's command before acting on impressions to do good deeds.

For behold, it is not meet that I should command in all
things;...

Verily I say, men should be anxiously engaged in a good cause,
and do many things of their own free will, and bring to pass
much righteousness;

For the power is in them—wherein they are agents unto
themselves. And inasmuch as men do good they shall in nowise
lose their reward. [D&C 58:26-28]

How wonderful to know we have power in our day to bring to
pass righteousness. Nephi summed it up by writing, "And it came
to pass that I, Nephi, beheld the power of the Lamb of God, that it
descended upon the saints of the church of the Lamb, and upon the
covenant people of the Lord, who were scattered upon all the face
of the earth; and they were armed with righteousness and with the
power of God in great glory" (1 Nephi 14:14).

May we not only be mindful of the power of God's glory, but
may we utilize it to share His love and His gospel throughout the
world.

For additional insight see the following:

- Robert D. Hales, "When Thou Art Converted, Strengthen Thy Brethren,"
  Ensign, May 1997, 80-83.
- Jeffrey R. Holland, "The Grandeur of God," *Ensign*, November 2003, 70-72.
- Russell M. Ballard, "Let Our Voices Be Heard," *Ensign*, May 2003, 16-18.

And I was led by the Spirit,
not knowing beforehand
the things which I should do.
1 Nephi 4:6

Led by the  Spirit

When Nephi said the covenant people of the Lord will be "armed with righteousness and with the power of God in great glory," (1 Nephi 14:14), it's clear he was inspired. His ability to foresee our day was a gift of the Spirit, which he cultivated early in his ministry. Although he described himself as "being exceedingly young" he had "great desires to know of the mysteries of God" so he prayed earnestly "unto the Lord; and behold [the Lord] did visit [Nephi]" (1 Nephi 2:16). Then Nephi was blessed to be "led by the Spirit, not knowing beforehand the things which [he] should do" (1 Nephi 4:6). Because Nephi delighted in pondering the things of eternal significance, it helped him stay close to the Spirit of the Lord throughout his life. "Behold my soul delighteth in the things of the Lord; and my heart pondereth continually upon the things which I have seen and heard" (2 Nephi 4:16).

To ponder *continually* may seem extreme. But don't worry. It won't be boring, although the older I get the harder it is to stay awake when I ponder. Therefore, I do my best meditating while walking or hiking. The gospel is multi-faceted with countless topics to ponder around the clock. If Nephi could do it, so can we.

When we do make time to meditate, we reap benefits and blessings as Nephi did.

Reaping is good. If I plant carrot seeds in my garden, I reap carrots. If I plant zucchinis, I get zucchinis. Boy, do I get zucchinis! If I plant nothing, do I get nothing? No, I get weeds. Therefore, I must continually ponder the things of God to plant good seeds in my spirit's soil so weeds won't grow. Staying in tune with the Holy Ghost will nourish those seeds until they flourish.

Pondering and Meditation

Is pondering really that ponderous? No. I believe it's a blessing. Meditation is medication for the spirit. The Prophet David O. McKay taught the value of meditation, as follows:

> I think we pay too little attention to the value of meditation, a principle of devotion. In our worship there are two elements: One is spiritual communion arising from our own meditation; the other, instruction from others, particularly from those who have authority to guide and instruct us. Of the two, the more profitable introspectively is the meditation. Meditation is the language of the soul. It is defined as "a form of private devotion, or spiritual exercise, consisting in deep, continued reflection on some religious theme." Meditation is a form of prayer....
> Meditation is one of the most secret, most sacred doors through which we pass into the presence of the Lord. Jesus set the example for us. [Conference Report, April 1946, 113]

Jesus used meditation and prayer before he called his Twelve (Luke 6:12-13), after feeding the five thousand, (Matthew 14:23), and in Gethsemane (Mark 14:32-40). He also invited the Nephites to gain strength through pondering. "I perceive that ye are weak, that ye cannot understand all my words which I am commanded of the Father to speak unto you at this time.

"Therefore, go ye unto your homes, and ponder upon the things which I have said, and ask of the Father, in my name, that ye may understand, and prepare your minds for the morrow, and I come unto you again" (3 Nephi 17:2-3).

In these latter days, we are also encouraged to reflect upon the words of God. "I leave these sayings with you to ponder in your hearts, with this commandment which I give unto you, that ye shall call upon me while I am near—" (D&C 88:62). One of the major ways The Church of Jesus Christ of Latter-day Saints differs from other religions is in the gift of the Holy Ghost. Through the Spirit's influence, we can receive personal revelation to guide our daily thoughts and actions. Sudden inspired thoughts, dreams, visions, and other spiritual manifestations have been given to worthy individuals throughout earth's history.

Joseph Smith received many of the revelations recorded in the Doctrine and Covenants as a result of his pondering the scriptures. An illustrious vision of the spirit world was also given to President Joseph F. Smith, who said, "As I pondered over these things which are written, the eyes of my understanding were opened, and the Spirit of the Lord rested upon me" (D&C 138:11). All of us can learn by the Spirit when we spend adequate time pondering the things of God.

Still Small Voice

One of my favorite prophets of the Old Testament is Elijah, who was not very popular with the rulers or common people in his time. When his life was in danger because of the wickedness around him, he had to flee for safety. Once he became so discouraged and isolated that he asked the Lord to take away his life. God sent an angel to comfort him with food and water, after which Elijah found a cave in which to dwell. While there, the word of the Lord came to him, saying, "Go forth, and stand upon the mount before the Lord. And, behold, the Lord passed by, and a great and strong wind rent the mountains, and brake in pieces the rocks before the Lord; but the Lord was not in the wind: and after the wind an earthquake; but the Lord was not in the earthquake:

"And after the earthquake a fire; but the Lord was not in the fire: and after the fire a still small voice" (1 Kings 19:11-12).

Elijah's faith must have been fine-tuned. He had already traveled a long way, but he left his safe cave to climb to the top of a mountain. Then he endured the three-pronged turmoil of wind, earthquake, and fire upon the mount. But somehow he remained steadfast and unshakeable. Despite the tumult, his ears were attuned to to hear the still small voice.

For the sake of brevity, I've heard people refer to the still small voice as SSV. That's not to be confused with an SUV. An SUV is driven by people on outings away from home. In contrast, the SSV drives people homeward to heaven.

One handicap for human beings is our inability to hear the Holy Spirit's whisperings above the ruckus of the world. With radio, television, CD's, DVD's, ipods, Internet, movies, traffic, sirens, and general chaos in day-to-day living, it's rare to find the silence or solitude necessary to ponder. Elder Boyd K. Packer echoed the need to utilize the gift of the Holy Ghost in this chaotic world:

> With all that is happening and with all the impossible challenges we face, we have that supernal gift of the Holy Ghost conferred upon us. And yet, for the most part, we know it not. It's interesting how in our lives, we are operating, to an extent, as though we had not received it....
> Change your lives and admit the inspiration of the Holy ghost. Begin to get your feelings sensitive enough so that you can be guided. You will not be denied!" ["And They Knew It Not," CES Fireside, 5 March 2000]

Personal Revelation

A mistake I often make is asking for personal revelation too late. Then I must beg for guidance *after* I'm already stuck in the middle of something. How much more prepared I'd be if I sought guidance in advance for the best thing to do in a situation. Then I wouldn't be saying, "Oops! What's the *second* best thing to do?"

The Holy Ghost can inspire our simple day-to-day routines. I will never forget a time when I was eight years old that my mother received a quiet urging to check on my sleeping baby brother.

In the midst of sewing, she initially resisted the thought. Then a second impulse jolted her, and she quickly stood up. Rushing to the nursery, she discovered the baby in danger. Somehow his blanket had become tightly wrapped around his head. He could barely breathe. Untangling the blanket, my mother saw his face had turned blue. She lifted him to her shoulder and patted his back. He let out a wail, and pink returned to his cheeks. None of our family had ever been so happy to hear him cry.

On the other hand, that doesn't mean my friend who lost a baby to Sudden Infant Death Syndrome wasn't in tune with the Holy Ghost. Questioning why she didn't receive a warning to check on her sleeping child only magnified her anguish. So, during her mourning, rather than wallowing in sorrow, she put her trust in the Lord. The whisperings of the Spirit brought peace to her soul and amplified her faith in Christ's Atonement and resurrection. She then was blessed with added wisdom and strength to carry on mothering her four living children.

Our Father in Heaven does not withhold inspiration simply because we aren't among a chosen few. Elder Bruce R. McConkie attested that righteous individuals are equally qualified to receive spiritual gifts.

> "Where spiritual things are concerned, as pertaining to all of the gifts of the Spirit, with reference to the receipt of revelation, the gaining of testimonies, and the seeing of visions, in all matters that pertain to godliness and holiness and which are brought to pass as a result of personal righteousness—in all these things men and women stand in a position of absolute equality before the Lord. He is no respecter of persons nor of sexes, and he blesses those men and those women who seek him and serve him and keep his commandments. ["Our Sisters from the Beginning," *Ensign*, Jan. 1979, p. 6]

Using Spiritual Inspiration

As we learn to attune our spirits, hearken, and carry forth divine directions, we will be given added ability to heed and proceed in matters of more importance. As Elder Neal A. Maxwell said, "God does not begin by asking us about our ability, but only about our availability, and if we then prove our dependability, he will increase our capability!" (*The Neal A. Maxwell Quote Book*, 1)

When inspired by the Holy Ghost, we are led to accomplish that which we otherwise may have been unaware. While serving a mission in London, England, one of our nephews received divine guidance, which he shared in the following e-mail:

> We prayed as to where we should go with what short time we had before an appointment in Abington.... We prayed about Wycliffe Road in particular, but I felt prompted to go to a street that ran perpendicular. I've learned that the best thing to do is to follow promptings when they come. So we tracted there. We met a young man from China ... who didn't know any English at all. Elder Parkinson only remembered how to say hello from when he taught some Chinese investigators in Duston.... So we just gave him an internet card and went on our way as he was able to explain that he flies back [to China] today. It then occurred to me that he would have no way to access the website thanks to the communist firewall. It then occurred to Elder Parkinson that there was an oriental language Book of Mormon in the van that hadn't been picked up by anyone. Lo and behold—Chinese! The gospel continues to penetrate the East. "By small and simple things...." [Marc Dotson, "Conversion is Consecration," 29 Sept. 2004]

Through their priesthood ordinations, ancient and Latter-day Prophets have been given unique abilities to communicate with the Spirit of the Lord. Only the President of the Church, whom we sustain as prophet, seer, and revelator, can reveal God's word for the Church in its entirety. Although the scope of this guidance is enormous—for all God's children—the main means of delivering divine messages is through the whisperings of the Spirit. Most revelation, even for prophets, is not given amid the dramatic events

Elijah experienced while upon a mountain. President Spencer W. Kimball explained it in this manner:

> The burning bushes, the smoking mountains,... the Cumorahs, and the Kirtlands were realities; but they were the exceptions. The great volume of revelation came to Moses and to Joseph and comes to today's prophet in the less spectacular way—that of deep impressions, without spectacle or glamour or dramatic events.
>
> Always expecting the spectacular, many will miss entirely the constant flow of revealed communication. [Spencer W. Kimball, Conference Report, Munich Germany Area Conference, 1973, 77]

Heart and Mind

Inspiration from the Holy Ghost comes to both the heart and mind. The Lord said, "Behold, I will tell you in your mind and in your heart, by the Holy Ghost, which shall come upon you and which shall dwell in your heart.

"Now, behold, this is the spirit of revelation; behold, this is the spirit by which Moses brought the children of Israel through the Red Sea on dry ground" (D&C 8:2-3).

Elder Jeffrey R. Holland quoted the above scripture, then went on to provide a wonderful treatise on personal revelation:

> I love the combination there of both mind and heart. God will teach us in a reasonable way and in a revelatory way—mind and heart combined by the Holy Ghost....
>
> Question: Why would the Lord use the example of crossing the Red Sea as the classic example of the "spirit of revelation"? Why didn't he use the First Vision?... Or the vision of the brother of Jared?
>
> Usually we think of revelation as information....
>
> First of all, revelation almost always comes in response to a question, usually an urgent question—not always, but usually....

You will need information, too, but in matters of great consequence it is not likely to come unless you want it urgently, faithfully, humbly. Moroni calls it seeking "with real intent" (Moroni 10:4)....

That is lesson number one about crossing the Red Sea, your Red Seas, by the spirit of revelation....

Lesson number two is closely related to it. It is that in the process of revelation and in making important decisions, fear almost always plays a destructive, sometimes paralyzing role....

That is the second lesson of the spirit of revelation. After you have gotten the message, after you have paid the price to feel his love and hear the word of the Lord, "go forward." Don't fear, don't vacillate, don't quibble, don't whine....

The third lesson from the Lord's spirit of revelation in the miracle of the crossing of the Red Sea is that, *along with the illuminating revelation that points us toward a righteous purpose or duty, God will also provide the means and power to achieve that purpose.* ["Cast Not Away Therefore Your Confidence," BYU Devotional, 2 March 1999, italics in the original]

Those inspired words invoke confidence that God is aware of each individual. He is able to give us the spiritual gifts necessary to succeed, if we willingly obey Him and exercise faith. Through the Spirit, the Lord provides us power beyond our human limitations. Elder Richard G. Scott emphasized this in a general conference address:

Joseph Smith was helped to accomplish tasks that were completely beyond his personal capacity. At times, this came through direct guidance and intervention. Yet often it was the quiet prompting of the Spirit and the accompanying support that came because of his obedience, his faith in the Master, and his unwavering determination to do His will....

I testify that within your own personal sphere of activity and framework of responsibilities, the Lord will provide that same help. When needed and earned, you can enjoy divine inspiration to know what to do and, when necessary, power or capacity to accomplish it. ["He Lives," *Ensign*, Nov. 1999, 89]

It has been a popular notion for people to take "power naps" to sharpen intellectual acuity. Perhaps it would be more beneficial to utilize "power surges" from the Holy Ghost, as Joseph Smith taught:

This first Comforter or Holy Ghost has no other effect than pure intelligence. It is more powerful in expanding the mind, enlightening the understanding, and storing the intellect with present knowledge,...

A person may profit by noticing the first intimation of the spirit of revelation; for instance, when you feel pure intelligence flowing into you, it may give you sudden strokes of ideas, so that by noticing it, you may find it fulfilled the same day or soon; (i.e.) those things that were presented unto your minds by the Spirit of God, will come to pass; and thus by learning the Spirit of God and understanding it, you may grow into the principle of revelation, until you become perfect in Christ Jesus. [*Teachings of the Prophet Joseph Smith*, 149, 151]

An Answer to Prayer

I hope you won't mind if I tell of a time when my heartfelt prayers were answered with a spiritual manifestation. I rarely share this story because it's difficult to write about with proper humility—I don't want it to sound trite and inconsequential. I'm not sure why I was blessed with this guidance, while some people struggle for years without clear answers to their prayers. But I'm grateful it happened to me.

During the summer of 1968, before leaving home for college in Logan, Utah, I spent more time in prayer than ever before in my life. Suddenly I was eighteen and expected to act somewhat like an adult. Wisdom is what I needed. Wiz-dumb is how I felt. I wasn't stupid by any means. I'd received a scholarship to Utah

State University. Hence, that summer before leaving for college, I often prayed for help with my college studies so I might keep the scholarship all four years. However, my chief concern at the time was for guidance to find an eternal companion.

Being a serious student, I'd had little high school experience in dating, dancing, or other social interactions with young men. Therefore, I earnestly prayed that I would find a man to love and cherish throughout eternity. I knew I didn't want the "till death do you part" kind of marriage. I didn't want to be like the wife who said, "My husband and I married for better or worse. He couldn't have done better than to wed me. And I couldn't have done worse."

My nightly petitions to God must have wearied Him halfway through the summer, because He finally responded to my pleas. After rising from my knees one night, I crawled into bed and closed my eyes. Instantly, my mind was caught up to view an inspired dream. I was not asleep, but fully aware of two distinct scenes displayed in my mind.

In the first setting, I saw myself dusting a desk in a bedroom. As I looked over my shoulder, there was a young man sitting on a double bed with books spread out for studying. He seemed to be of average height, he had a kind face, brown curly hair, and broad shoulders.

The second panorama I viewed was set in nature. I stood on a grassy slope among aspen trees to overlook a small lake. Between me and the water was a young man, who appeared taller than the first one I'd seen. His back was toward me, so I didn't see his face. I could only note that he had blond hair and an athletic build. The most intriguing part of the scene was that my hand reached toward him, as if I wanted to make him turn around and look at me.

That was all. Two young men in two different settings. Yet it left an impression in my soul that is as clear now as when it happened. I knew I'd be searching to find these two handsome hombres when I attended Utah State University.

My very first week on campus in our student ward, I sat at the rear of the chapel and stared at a blond young man. He was on the first row among other priesthood holders who would pass the sacrament. Sunday after Sunday he sat there for me to see. Each week I became more convinced this was the second young man I'd seen in my dream. But I never had an opportunity to meet him face to face. However, I did find out his name and looked up information about him in the student directory. I discovered he'd grown up in Parowan, Utah, as one of nine children. I was naive enough about "boys" that I actually toyed with the idea of writing a letter to his mother to say I was dying to meet her son! Thank goodness I didn't do it.

November came, and after the first blizzard blew through town, I trudged outside with my roommates to play in the snow. Soon we were tossing snowballs with some young men from a neighboring dorm. Before long, the frivolity wore out our arms, and the winter chill seeped through our clothes to make us shiver. We invited the guys into our dorm's social room for hot chocolate. After the cocoa and mini marshmallows disappeared, along with a few stale cookies, the students began to leave. One by one, they made excuses about homework or fatigue and departed, except for me and a fellow named Jerry.

As we sat on a couch to chat, I noticed his broad shoulders, curly brown hair, and kind face. My heart zinged with sudden recognition. Jerry was the first young man I'd seen in my dream! As might be expected, we began to date. We played guitars, hiked, laughed, and occasionally studied together at the library. More than once he took me home to Smithfield, north of Logan, for Sunday dinners with his family. During the Christmas holidays, he came to Salt Lake City to meet my family.

January classes began before I knew it, and once again I saw the blond-headed priest sitting on the front row at Church. To my delight, I discovered he was also in my botany class! Somehow, I knew I couldn't get serious with Jerry until I became acquainted with this other young man. Though my dream had shown it was my responsibility to reach out in his direction, I remained reluctant.

In late January, Utah State was scheduled to play basketball against the University of Utah, so I invited three high school girl friends, who now attended the U of U, to come stay in Logan with me for the weekend. I don't remember which team won the game, but I do remember going with my friends to the dance afterward. During a lull, we went to relax in a quiet spot and chat about school and the "opposite sex." When I mentioned I had my eye on someone from Parowan, one of my friends said, "Oh, I have relatives in Parowan! I go there to visit my grandparents all the time! I might know this guy. What's his name?"

When I divulged his name, Glenn Robinson (which is a clue to how this story ends), she exclaimed, "That's my first cousin! His mom is my dad's sister. He's smart, but he's really, really shy." I didn't care if he was shy, except that it explained why he'd been rather hard to meet.

The next day at church, my friend introduced me to her cousin Glenn. If I'd dared, I would have let loose with a Tarzan yell! Though we had but a moment to chat at that time, it gave me enough fortitude to sit by him the next day in botany class.

We'd been given a test on the previous Friday, and when the professor began to hand back our papers, Glenn volunteered to pick mine up for me. As he returned to his seat beside me, I saw his score was 88% and mine 92%. Not wanting that to be a "turn off" for him, I hastily asked him to come to dinner on Thursday evening. He accepted, and we had our first "date" together with my five roommates.

The next week I invited him to our dorm's formal dance to celebrate Valentine's Day. As I look back, I was rather pushy with him. But I kept remembering my dream that implied I had to be the one to reach out and get the relationship going. Well, this shy guy finally got the not-too-subtle message I was sending, and the next Saturday he asked me to go bowling. Funny, I outscored him by forty points (due to my taking a bowling class that quarter). Nonetheless, he began to ask me out regularly.

Of course, I had to juggle time spent with Glenn against my outings with Jerry. I couldn't believe it! Dates coming at me right and left! This just wasn't like me! As winter quarter dwindled to a close, I began to see less of Jerry.

Glenn, on his way home to Parowan for spring break, made a brief stop at my house in Salt Lake City. I'll never forget what my youngest brother said after the introductions: "I like you better than the last guy she brought home."

Before long, both Jerry and Glenn went on missions and wrote me faithfully. I'll bet you can guess which one received a "Dear John" letter halfway through his mission. Anyway, I think you get the picture. I hope you also get the bigger picture, that despite my being but an ordinary eighteen-year-old, God was mindful of me and my future. I'm still not sure why the Spirit of the Lord blessed me so profoundly with a dream that shaped the rest of my life. But I am eternally grateful for the inspiration I received.

Glenn and I have now been married for thirty-four years, which is somewhat miraculous in this divorce-riddled world. Don't believe what you may have heard, that "a man in love is incomplete until he's married. Then he's finished." With an eternal perspective, marriage is just the beginning of our human stretch toward godhood.

Be Prayerful

The prayers of the righteous can yield inspired actions, prompted by the Holy Ghost. Often, revelation is a result of prayer and fasting, as Alma attested, "Behold, I say unto you they are made known unto me by the Holy Spirit of God. Behold, I have fasted and prayed many days that I might know these things of myself. And now I do know of myself that they are true; for the Lord God hath made them manifest unto me by his Holy Spirit; and this is the spirit of revelation which is in me" (Alma 5:46).

There's nothing so phenomenal as prayer power. Of course, it may not help you prepare your Sunday School lesson while attending a Saturday night motorcycle rally. But when conditions are conducive to the Spirit, you can be inspired, instructed, guided, enlightened, edified, protected, comforted, and purified through manifestations of the Holy Ghost.

Although it's best to pray in a tranquil setting, most of us have issued prayers in our hearts while in the midst of the jungle of life. Whether infested by tarantulas, coiled by boa constrictors, or stalked by panthers, our daily lives can be blessed by the comforting presence of the Spirit.

The best part about calling upon God is that He will personally listen every time you speak to Him. He doesn't employ a secretary or have an answering machine. He won't screen anyone out by using caller I.D. Nor does He refuse telephone solicitors. In fact, our Father welcomes all solicitations and pleas that come His way.

Blessings of the Holy Spirit

The Holy Spirit has inspired people to perform good works through all the ages of time. It benefits everyone, whether they are members of the Church or not. The Spirit's influence can enlighten a person before baptism to witness that the gospel is true. However, the "gift" of the constant companionship of the Holy Ghost is more discretional. It is offered after baptism through the laying on of hands by a man ordained to the Melchizedek priesthood. Since this confirmation is often given to a child at the tender age of eight, its importance may be overlooked. Yet receiving the Holy Ghost should be a very sacred moment—whether at the accountable age of eight or at a later stage of life.

During this priesthood ordinance, we are instructed "receive the Holy Ghost," meaning it's up to us as individuals to keep the channel of inspiration open. Each worthy child of God will be given as much of the Spirit as he or she seeks through faith and prayer. Whether we're baptized as eight-year-olds, teenagers, or adults, it doesn't matter. Whether or not we eat our vegetables isn't taken into account. Only our righteousness and faithfulness will be weighed in receiving the constant conpanionship of the Holy Ghost.

Unlike the spam and junk mail that often pops into my e-mail inbox, the Holy Ghost provides uplifting and edifying information. No scams to worry about. You can trust your life with this member of the Godhead. Indeed, that is what we must do—trust.

I like the play on words here. Trust means to have confidence in something, or to rely on someone. But Webster's dictionary also defines it in legal terms, as "a right or interest in property held by one person for the benefit of another." In this case, the Holy Ghost is the trustee, holding "property" for the benefit of God's children. As the "trustors," we are endowed with gifts and blessings through the Spirit. Because the functions of the Holy Ghost are many, I will pinpoint only a few herein:

1. The Holy Ghost bears witness of Heavenly Father and Jesus Christ. "For behold, the Comforter knoweth all things, and beareth record of the Father and of the Son" (D&C 42:17).

2. The Holy Ghost is a teacher, revealing the truth of all things. "But the Comforter, which is the Holy Ghost,... shall teach you all things, and bring all things to your remembrance" (John 14:26). "And by the power of the Holy Ghost ye may know the truth of all things" (Moroni 10:5).

3. The Holy Ghost improves our bodies and our intellects, as Parley P. Pratt observed:

The gift of the Holy Spirit adapts itself to all these organs or attributes. It quickens all the intellectual faculties, increases, enlarges, expands, and purifies all the natural passions and affections, and adapts them, by the gift of wisdom, to their lawful use. It inspires, develops, cultivates, and matures all the fine-toned sympathies, joys, tastes, kindred feelings, and affections of our nature. It inspires virtue, kindness, goodness, tenderness, gentleness, and charity. It develops beauty of person, form and features. It tends to health, vigor, animation, and social feeling. It develops and invigorates all the faculties of the physical and intellectual man. It strengthens, invigorates, and gives tone to the nerves. In short, it is, as it were, marrow to the bone, joy to the heart, light to the eyes, music to the ears, and life to the whole being. [*Key to the Science of Theology*, 101]

4. The Holy Ghost sanctifies those who have repented and been baptized. "Repent, . . . and be baptized in my name, that ye may be sanctified by the reception of the Holy Ghost, that ye may stand spotless before me at the last day" (3 Nephi 27:20).

5. The Holy Ghost allows us to speak with the tongue of angels. In a discourse on the doctrine of Christ that includes baptism and receipt of the Holy Ghost, Nephi wrote:

Do ye not remember that I said unto you that after ye had received the Holy Ghost ye could speak with the tongue of angels? And now, how could ye speak with the tongue of angels save it were by the Holy Ghost?
Angels speak by the power of the Holy Ghost;… they speak the words of Christ. Wherefore, I said unto you, feast upon the words of Christ; for behold, the words of Christ will tell you all things what ye should do" (2 Nephi 32:2-3).

Gifts of the Spirit

Life would be simpler if we could truly utilize the power of the Holy Ghost and hearken to the words of Christ that tell us everything we should do. Often, we're caught amid the grinding gears of daily life in what seems to be an obstacle course. But don't get confused. This is not an Olympic-style competition, where only one person can win the coveted gold medal. Never forget, in the decathlon events of earthly life and the marathon races toward celestial life, we do not compete against anyone but ourselves. In all our efforts to be the best of the best, we will be individually appraised and awarded. All God's children can achieve the victory of a celestial medal, if they strive for it. However, some may only live worthy of terrestrial or telestial rewards.

Our progress toward exaltation is better accomplished when we utilize the gifts of the Spirit. Some of these are specified in Article of Faith 7, "We believe in the gift of tongues, prophecy, revelation, visions, healing, interpretation of tongues, and so forth." Broader references to spiritual gifts are found in Section 46 of the Doctrine and Covenants, chapter 12 of First Corinthians, and chapter 10 of Moroni. However, these are not complete listings of all the gifts we can seek, as Elder Bruce R. McConkie explained:

"The gifts of the Spirit are for believing, faithful, righteous people; they are reserved for the saints of God. They come from God in heaven to man on earth in a miraculous manner. Their receipt is a miracle, and faith precedes the miracle....
"Spiritual gifts are endless in number and infinite in variety" (*A New Witness for the Articles of Faith*, 370-371).

Though these miraculous gifts are available from God to benefit His children on earth, some people lack desire for such heaven-sent blessings. But then, mankind can be a curious bunch to figure out. When anyone claims it's impossible to lick your own elbow, most of us instantly try to prove the statement wrong.

Whether or not people realize it, admit it, utilize it, or bless others' lives with it, everyone possesses at least one gift of the Spirit. Scriptures state that "to every man is given a gift by the Spirit of God.

"To some is given one, and to some is given another, that all may be profited thereby" (D&C 46:11-12).

We can perfect our own lives, and thus benefit other children of God through seeking after these things (see Article of Faith 13). Ponder this wonderful insight from Elder George Q. Cannon:

I feel to bear testimony to you, my brethren and sisters,... that God is the same today as He was yesterday; that God is willing to bestow these gifts upon His children.... If any of us are imperfect, it is our duty to pray for the gift that will make us perfect.... God has promised to give the gifts that are necessary for [our] perfection." [*Millennial Star* 56, April 1894, 260-61]

Conclusion

The Holy Ghost can bless our lives in countless ways. With no physical body, the Spirit can actually dwell in our hearts, for "the Holy Ghost has not a body of flesh and bones, but is a personage of Spirit. Were it not so, the Holy Ghost could not dwell in us" (D&C 130:22). God the Father, Jesus Christ, and the Holy Ghost have perfect "oneness" in the Godhead. Therefore, if the Holy Ghost dwells in you, isn't that nearly equivalent to Heavenly Father or Jesus Christ dwelling within you?

After Joseph Smith's death, Brigham Young reported a vision he'd seen of the martyred prophet. Brigham immediately asked if Joseph had a word of counsel for him. Of all the messages Joseph might have delivered, he choose to expound upon the necessity of keeping the Spirit of the Lord.

> Tell the people to be humble and faithful, and be sure to keep the Spirit of the Lord and it will lead them right. Be careful and not turn away the small, still voice; it will teach them what to do and where to go; it will yield the fruit of the kingdom. Tell the brethren to keep their hearts open to conviction, so that when the Holy Ghost comes to them, their hearts will be ready to receive it. They can tell the Spirit of the Lord from all other spirits, it will whisper peace and joy to their souls; it will take malice, hatred, strife and all evil from their hearts; and their whole desire will be to do good, bring forth righteousness and build up the Kingdom of God. Tell the brethren if they will follow the Spirit of the Lord, they will go right. Be sure to tell the people to keep the Spirit of the Lord. [*Manuscript History of Brigham Young*, Feb. 23, 1847]

Joseph Smith appeared from heavenly realms to render this concise counsel to keep the Spirit. Shall we not devote prayer and energy to pursuing this goal? Brigham Young endeavored to teach this doctrine after hearing Joseph's counsel:

Without the power of the Holy Ghost a person is liable to go
to the right or the left from the straight path of duty ...
I want to see men and women breathe the Holy Ghost in
every breath of their lives, living constantly in the light of
God's countenance." [*Discourses of Brigham Young 9:288-289*,
arranged by John A. Widtsoe, 1954, 31]

What a potent statement that we should "breathe the Holy
Ghost in every breath of [our] lives." How blessed God's children
would be to live in such a manner! How blessed the entire world
would be! Everyone can benefit by Elder Marion G. Romney's
words, "When we learn to distinguish between the inspiration
that comes from the Spirit of the Lord and that which comes from
our own uninspired hopes and desires, we need make no mistakes.
To this I testify" ("I Have a Question," *New Era*, Oct. 1975, 35).

For additional insight see:

- Dallin H. Oaks, "I Have A Question," *Ensign*, June 1983, 27.
- Bruce R. McConkie, "Spiritual Gifts," *A New Witness for the Articles of Faith*,
  366-377.
- Robert L. Millet, *Alive in Christ: The Miracle of Spiritual Rebirth*, Salt Lake
  City, Deseret Book Co., 1997.
- Boyd K. Packer "And They Knew It Not," CES Fireside, 5 March 2000.
- Richard G. Scott, "He Lives," *Ensign*, Nov. 1999, 87-90.
- Jeffrey R. Holland, "Cast Not Away Therefore Your Confidence," BYU
  Devotional, 2 March 1999.
- Robert L. Millet, *Alive in Christ: The Miracle of Spiritual Rebirth*, Salt Lake
  City, Deseret Book Co., 1997, 203.

Verily, verily, I say unto you, this is my gospel;
and ye know the things that ye must do in my church;
for the works which ye have seen me do,
that shall ye also do.
3 Nephi 27:21

Know the Things You Must Do

What better way to live than emulating Jesus Christ? We can never learn too much about His example and teachings. In our pre-earthly existence, Jesus offered Himself in consummate service to our Father by saying: "Here am I, send me" (Abraham 3:27). Near the end of His mortal life, He reported, "I have glorified thee on the earth: I have finished the work which thou gavest me to do" (John 17:4). Then, with His final breath, He said, "Father, into thy hands I commend my spirit" (Luke 23:46).

To duplicate the righteous works of Jesus and finish the work our Father gave us to do, we must also say, "Here am I, send me." I wonder, too, if it's possible to commend our spirits into our Father's keeping—not just after death, but right now.

After His resurrection and ascension to heaven, Jesus spent several days with Lehi's descendants. Toward the end of His time in the Promised Land, He said with authority, "Verily, verily, I say unto you, this is my gospel; and ye know the things that ye must do in my church; for the works which ye have seen me do that shall ye also do; for that which ye have seen me do even that shall ye do" (3 Nephi 27:21).

Doing what Jesus Christ has done means that we're committed to the will of the Father. "If any man will do his will, he shall know of the doctrine, whether it be of God, or whether I speak of myself" (John 7:17). We are not required to follow nebulous or ridiculous doctrines, but the truth as it has been spoken by our Father since before the foundation of the world. Through ancient scripture and modern-day revelation, we have the words of God to guide our thoughts and behavior.

Keep The Commandments

Perhaps the most universally known words of God are the Ten Commandments in Exodus 20:3-17. Though these laws are precise and succinct, some people attempt to bend and twist them to serve their own purposes. For example, they might contend that "thou shalt not bear false witness" (Exodus 20:16) does not specifically say "do not lie," "don't tell half-truths," or "don't hide the truth by not speaking."

I recall a day my son and his girlfriend were on their way to the neighborhood swimming club. I asked if he had $2.00 to pay his date's fee, since she was not a member of the club.

He said, "Last time we went no one asked us to pay."

As a mother often does, I seized the teaching moment. "No one ever asks you to pay. It's just expected. It's the honest thing to do. She's not a member of the swim club, and $2.00 is not much to ask in return for a clear conscience." Without another word, my son went back inside to get his wallet.

Sometimes God's children need precise explanations about proper conduct. That seems true in recent years during general conference addresses. Specific instructions have been given to stay out of debt, and to avoid drugs, pornography, tattoos, and body piercings. We're also frequently counseled to become more prepared for the Last Days. That means temporal readiness through maintaining a year's supply of food, clothing, and fuel. Also we should have an adequate storage of water or a means to purify nearby sources of water. Building and maintaining a spiritual reservoir to combat latter-day turmoil is also crucial. Faithfully studying the scriptures, praying with heart-felt intent, attending church meetings, repentance, forgiveness, temple worship, and serving others will enhance our reservoir of sprituality. The list of positive behavior for Latter-day Saints to develop is quite extensive. But I hope we will never require such tedious details of conduct as Moses had to give the Israelites in Leviticus and Deuteronomy.

I suppose you've heard the religious jokes that say the reason the Israelites wandered for forty years in the wilderness was that, like some macho men, Moses wouldn't ask for directions. Also it was difficult to see at night, for all Moses had to light the way was "Israel-lights." Putting humor aside, the truth is, Moses consistently asked the Lord for guidance for his people. Yet the Israelites often murmured against divine counsel and continued clinging to Egyptian values.

Just to clarify, Moses and his people did have God directing their pathway by night and day. "And the Lord went before them by day in a pillar of a cloud, to lead them in the way; and by night in a pillar of fire, to give them light; to go by day and night (Exocus 13:21). Still, many Israelites failed to let the light into their souls.

When itemized directions are given of what to do and what not to do, that's the letter of the law. When we follow the quiet promptings in our hearts, that's the spirit of the law. Occasionally people feel compelled to obey laws out of fear of punishment or because others are watching. In contrast, ponder the example of Adam, who "was obedient unto the commandments of the Lord.

"And after many days an angel of the Lord appeared unto Adam, saying: Why dost thou offer sacrifices unto the Lord? And Adam said unto him: I know not, save the Lord commanded me" (Moses 5:5-6).

Adam was obedient for the mere reason that the Lord gave him commandments. He did not have to know the "why" behind each law of the gospel. Nor did he obey with the intent to be rewarded, though keeping commandments does bring blessings. "But learn that he who doeth the works of righteousness shall receive his reward, even peace in this world, and eternal life in the world to come" (D&C 59:23). Isn't peace in this world something humanity hungers for? And eternal life is greatest of all the gifts of God (D&C 14:7).

Sermon on the Mount

Christ's familiar Sermon on the Mount offers many suggestions of God-like characteristics. Our motivation for developing these virtues should be a desire to become more like our Heavenly Father and Jesus Christ. The principles are simple, yet profound. The more divine attributes we acquire, the nearer we come to eternal life and exaltation with the Father and Son. Because the beatitudes are further clarified in the Book of Mormon than in the Bible, I suggest a thorough study of 3 Nephi 12:2-12. All these characteristics and more can become inherent in us when we are "doers of the word, and not hearers only" (James 1:22). To be true doers and not just hearers, we must first understand the words of God to incorporate them into our daily lives.

From time to time I make checklists to assess my spiritual progress. Utilizing scriptures, I pinpoint qualities to develop in order to emulate Jesus Christ. I've discovered that it's rare, if not impossible, to incorporate all these traits at once. Most of them require a lifetime of practice. As always, our aim must exceed our grasp. After all, it's better to aim for the stars and miss, than to aim for a manure pile and hit.

Since attributes of godliness are numerous, I concentrate on certain ones at different stages in my life. I also take note of any promises offered within the verses I select—since blessings add incentive for self-improvement. In my scriptural lists, I usually change the pronouns to "I" to make them more personal. These endeavors are meant to be kept between me and my Father in Heaven. But I will share a few with you, if you promise not to throw tomatoes. That would stain the pages with red blotches and get your fingers all sticky. Consider these personalized verses:

From the Doctrine and Covenants 11:21—
I seek to obtain God's word that my tongue will be loosed.

I desire to have the Spirit and the power of God for convincing others of His word.

From the Doctrine and Covenants 18:10—
I remember the worth of souls is great in the sight of God.

From Mosiah 18:8-9, 20—
I am willing to bear other peoples' burdens.
I am willing to mourn with those that mourn, and comfort those that need comfort.
I will stand as a witness of God at all times, and in all things, and in all places that I am in, even until death.

From Mosiah 3:19—
I am learning to yield to the enticings of the Holy Spirit.
I will endeavor to put off the natural man.
I will become a saint through the Atonement of Christ.
I am becoming more childlike, submissive, meek, humble, patient, and full of love.

We'll pause with those few examples, because now you see how my checklist works. Perhaps you'd rather concentrate on your own spiritual goals. Most likely, you already have a temporal "to do list" similar to mine: Rotate the car's tires. Get a flu shot. Phone Aunt Bessie. Feed the dog. Wait a minute. I don't have a dog. Come to think of it, I don't have an Aunt Bessie either

Unlike our lists of earthly items to do, spiritual lists may require more thought and study, more consecration and energy. If, like me, you sometimes feel overwhelmed by scriptural requirements, remember Jesus said, "Pray always, that ye may not faint, until I come" (D&C 88:126).

Not faint. You betcha! Even with all my hefty lists and soul-stretching goals. So much to do, and so little time. But that's the secret! Because we don't have "all the time in the world," our maturing into godliness will continue into eternal life. I must say, *mature* isn't one of my favorite terms. It's in the same category as *old age* and *senior citizen.* That's why I often wear my t-shirt that says: "Young at heart! Slightly older other places!" Thankfully, spiritual maturity provides better rewards than physical aging.

Liken Scriptures Unto Us

When considering verses to guide my conduct, I appreciate Nephi's suggestion, to "liken all scriptures unto us, that it might be for our profit and learning" (1 Nephi 19:23). For example, I know where I stand regarding charity after studying Moroni 7:45-48. By pondering Matthew 5:44, I remember to I love my enemies and pray for those who persecute me. In my daily living, I make progress by doing as Nephi suggests, "we talk of Christ, we rejoice in Christ, we preach of Christ, and we write according to our prophecies [and testimonies] of Christ, that our children may know to what source they must look for a remission of their sins" (2 Nephi 25:26).

There are enumerable divine characteristics we can seek. Rather than listing each one for you, I suggest you settle with your scriptures into a cozy chair or hammock. If you're backpacking, go find a log to perch on. If you've just returned from skiing, perhaps you can relax in a warm bubble bath. But don't drop your scriptures in the water, or you can't study these references: Alma, Chapter 5; Mosiah, Chapter 4; Alma 7:22-24; Alma 37:33-36.

No matter at what rate you and I are progressing, it's good to concentrate on developing one godly attribute at a time. And remember to seek counsel from the Lord "in all thy doings, and he will direct thee for good" (Alma 37:37).

An Uphill Climb

Every few years I muster the courage to hike to the top of Mount Olympus on the eastern edge of the Salt Lake Valley. Reaching the summit requires a 4,200-foot elevation climb through four miles of switchbacks, steep trails, and, near the top, some scrambling up a trepidant rocky face. Many people stop at the "saddle" and do not attempt the last 400 feet to the peak. Each time I reach that spot, I waver with exhaustion and must force my shaky legs to continue.

As I slowly scale the craggy boulders, struggling to find secure hand and footholds, I try to convince myself that ascending is the difficult part, and then descending the trail later will be easier.

When finally I reach the peak of Mount Olympus, I spend time in awesome gazing at the expansive valley below. Then I take a few photos, eat a nourishing snack, and prepare to hike back down. As I study the steep terrain and descend only fifty feet, I find myself admitting that going downslope is much more perilous. Each shinny down the precipitous rocks purports a possible fall. As I cling with my hands and slide my feet toward hopeful toeholds, I wish I were still headed uphill. Though it may be more taxing to my muscles and my heart to ascend a steep incline, that produces less fear. And besides, going upward is far more rewarding since a specific goal is achieved by reaching the top.

A scenario can be drawn with our existence on earth. Often, humans seek the easiest way through life—not the one that comes with struggle. Indeed, we welcome the words of Christ: "For my yoke is easy, and my burden is light" (Matthew 11:30). Jesus doesn't mean that taking His yoke will be effortless, but that carrying the burdens of life *with Him* in our ascent heavenward is better than going it alone. Also it's easier to follow the path upward to heaven than to descend uncertain terrain and risk falling into the precarious pathways Satan offers.

For several days following a hike to Mount Olympus, the muscles in my legs are in rebellion. Every time I move, especially on staircases, I know I've strained my calves and thighs. Funny that my legs hurt the worst going downstairs, not up. That's another reminder that my energy is better used ascending toward a lofty celestial goal than descending toward a bottomless pit of darkness and evil. I like the way B. H. Roberts phrased this idea:

> If there is one struggle more than another in which the race is not to the swift nor the battle to the strong, but to those who endure to the end, it is in this struggle for eternal life....
>
> There is no one great thing that man can do and then do no more and obtain salvation. After entering into the kingdom of

God,... it is by learning "precept upon precept; line upon line; here a little and there a little" [Isaiah 28:10], that salvation will be made secure. It is by resisting temptation today, overcoming a weakness tomorrow.... Salvation is a matter of character-building under the Gospel laws and ordinances, and more especially with the direct aid of the Holy Spirit.

Nor is it enough that one get rid of evil. He must do good.... He must cultivate noble sentiments by performing noble deeds.... Every such deed performed with an eye single to the glory of God, draws one that much nearer into harmony with Deity. [*Gospel and Man's Relationship to Deity*, 208]

To reiterate, it's not enough for us to rid ourselves of evil. We must also set a course of positive performance in our attitudes and actions. That can be harder than it sounds, particularly with "opposition in all things" (see 2 Nephi 2:11). In opposing the Lord's work, Satan will do all he can to frustrate our noble efforts.

The Devil Is Real

Though not a pleasant topic to dwell upon, we must beware of the reality of Satan, who endeavors to thwart God's plan of salvation. The devil has great power, to which the Prophet Joseph Smith gave witness when he prayed in the Sacred Grove.

I kneeled down and began to offer up the desires of my heart to God. I had scarcely done so, when immediately I was seized upon by some power which entirely overcame me, and had such an astonishing influence over me as to bind my tongue so that I could not speak. Thick darkness gathered around me, and it seemed to me for a time as if I were doomed to sudden destruction.

But, exerting all my powers to call upon God to deliver me out of the power of this enemy,... not to an imaginary ruin, but to the power of some actual being from the unseen world, who had such marvelous power as I had never before felt in any being—just at this moment of great alarm, I saw a pillar of light exactly over my head. [JS–History 1:15-16]

This unseen and violent thrust of darkness seized Joseph Smith with a power beyond anything he could imagine. Similar evil forces also thrust themselves on Heber C. Kimball and his brethren while missionaries in England. During a general conference address 5 October 1896, President Wilford Woodruff retold Elder Kimball's experiences and related several of his own in dealing with the powers of Satan. I have no desire to dwell upon those eerie events—not in this book, nor in my personal life. Suffice it to quote President Woodruff's testimony from the pulpit:

There are two powers on the earth and in the midst of the inhabitants of the earth—the power of God and the power of the devil.... When God has had a people on the earth, it matters not in what age, Lucifer, the son of the morning, and the millions of fallen spirits that were cast out of heaven, have warred against God, against Christ, against the work of God, and against the people of God. [Brian H. Stuy, ed., *Collected Discourses*, vol. 5.]

Negativity and evil are not meant to dishearten, dissuade, or discourage us in doing the Lord's work. Rather, they warn us to be prayerful and watchful against the evil powers that continually strive to thwart God's eternal plan for His children. That these events are frightening and destructive is true. But God's power is far more potent than any evil being's. Our Father has endowed the righteous with courage to remain true to the faith, and He has provided priesthood powers to overcome Satan and his followers. The fact that you and I are on the earth is proof that we've already repelled the devil's threats in pre-earth life (see Abraham 3:24-28). If perchance Satan does try to deceive, tempt, or thwart your spiritual progress, think of this line I saw on a t-shirt: "If the devil reminds you of your past, you remind him of his future."

Within each of us is a divinely nurtured spirit that once resided in the presence of our Father. To give us added strength against evil forces, we have the light of the gospel, the influence of the Holy Ghost, the scriptures, and latter-day prophets and apostles. We also have a body of flesh and bone, which Satan and his followers will never receive. The Prophet Joseph Smith taught that "all beings who have bodies have power over those who have not" (*Teachings of the Prophet Joseph Smith,* 181).

If we, as children of God, have been blessed with such wonderful and innate power, it seems wise to cultivate a more celestial view of ourselves and those around us.

Through Spiritual Eyes

Many days we peer at our existence through a warped and worldly perspective. How grateful we are for occasional glimpses of life through a lens of spirituality. Perhaps you recall decades ago when there was a television series about a bionic man and a bionic woman. Their "bionic" enhancements made them more powerful than normal human beings. Some of those fictional ideas have actually come to pass, such as artificial hearts, and more recently, the development of an artificial hand that looks and functions like a real one. Today's scientists have created electronic devices to replicate human sight and hearing. Surgeons can replace worn out joints with mechanical hips and knees.

As a child, I used to dream I was Superman, flying to rescue anyone who needed my help. I'm not sure why I didn't dream I was Wonder Woman rather than a male superhero. At any rate, in my dreams, one super-human trick I enjoyed was the ability to see through walls and other blockades. Now as an adult, I long for the ability to see life more clearly through spiritual eyes.

Several scriptures tell of Jesus administering to blind individuals and restoring their sight. One record says Jesus "spat on the ground, and made clay of the spittle, and he anointed the eyes of the blind man with the clay" (John 9:6). After the man washed in the pool of Siloam, as Jesus instructed him, he was no longer blind. Wouldn't it be marvelous if the Savior could anoint our eyes with clay that we might have eternal sight and celestial perspective?

I'm intrigued with the account of Enoch, who was also asked to put clay on his eyes then wash them. Like Moses and Jonah, when the Lord addressed him from heaven and asked him to prophesy to the people, Enoch was hesitant to obey.

> And when Enoch had heard these words, he bowed himself to the earth, before the Lord, and spake before the Lord, saying: Why is it that I have found favor in thy sight, and am but a lad, and all the people hate me; for I am slow of speech; wherefore am I thy servant?
>
> And the Lord said unto Enoch: Go forth and do as I have commanded thee, and no man shall pierce thee. Open thy mouth, and it shall be filled, and I will give thee utterance, for all flesh is in my hands, and I will do as seemeth me good....
>
> Behold, my Spirit is upon you, wherefore all thy words will I justify; and the mountains shall flee before you, and the rivers shall turn from their course; and thou shalt abide in me, and I in you; therefore walk with me.
>
> And the Lord spake unto Enoch, and said unto him: Anoint thine eyes with clay, and wash them, and thou shalt see. And he did so.
>
> And he beheld the spirits that God had created; and he beheld also things which were not visible to the natural eye. [Moses 6:31-32, 34-36]

After much communing with God, Enoch became one of the most powerful men to ever walk the earth. Despite his initial feelings of inadequacy, he trusted in the Lord and exercised the faith necessary to boldly testify before the people. Perhaps the covering of Enoch's eyes with clay was symbolic of his focus on worldly concerns. Then by washing off the dust of the earth, his visual acuity cleared so he could view everything from God's perspective.

Of course, anointing eyes with clay and washing them is not the magic that provides celestial vision. It is the intensity of our faith in Jesus Christ that allows us to behold things not visible to the natural eye. Indeed, faith is not simply a desire or hope. It is power and energy focused with pure intent, as Joseph Smith taught:

> When a man works by faith he works by mental exertion instead of physical force. It is by words, instead of exerting his physical powers, with which every being works when he works by faith. God said, 'Let there be light: and there was light.... Faith, then, works by words; and with these its mightiest works have been, and will be, performed....
>
> The whole visible creation, as it now exists, is the effect of faith. It was faith by which it was framed, and it is by the power of faith that it continues in its organized form, and by which the planets move round their orbits and sparkle forth their glory. [*Lectures on Faith*, 72-73]

When men and women achieve exquisite faith, which can move mountains and create the cosmos, they are prepared to become gods. Until then, the children of God must seek for spiritual eyes, through which to view the eternal nature of all things.

Proving Ourselves

God has witnessed our lives since before we were born on earth. Being all-wise, He realized we might not measure up to all that's expected of us. So He prepared a way to redeem us through the Atonement of His Son, if we repent. God is omniscient. He already knows everything about you and me—how we will behave or misbehave in each situation life presents. As He said of all His children, "We will make an earth where on these may dwell;

"And we will prove them herewith, to see if they will do all things whatsoever the Lord their God shall command them;" (Abraham 3:24-25).

With His omniscience, God sees in advance how we will perform in every circumstance. Therefore, we are not here to prove to God something He already knows. Rather, we are here to prove to ourselves if we will do all the Lord commands us on our pathway to perfection, as Elder Bruce R. McConkie said:

> We have to become perfect to be saved in the celestial kingdom. But nobody becomes perfect in this life. [Yet] if we chart a course of sanctifying our souls, and degree by degree are going in [the right] direction; and if we chart a course of becoming perfect,... perfecting our souls by overcoming the world, then it is absolutely guaranteed—we shall gain eternal life.... We're not going to be perfect the minute we die. But if we've charted a course, if our desires are right,... and we are doing to the very best of our abilities what we ought to do, we'll go on to everlasting salvation. ["Jesus Christ and Him Crucified," *Devotional Speeches of the Year*, 399]

That in mind, I'll share with you a few more scriptures from my spiritual checklist. Of course you don't have to read them. No one is going to make you. At least not in this instant of time. But it's better to do it "in time" rather than in eternity. These verses have helped me assess my progress in my relationship to the Father and the Son: Proverbs 3:5; Matthew 16:24-25; John 8:12; John 17:3; Helaman 5:12; 2 Nephi 25:29; and Mosiah 5:12.

Conclusion

The scriptures provide a vast array of divine attributes and righteous behavior for us to develop. It's not enough to say, "I will try to do these things," or "I hope I can." A full commitment to God is necessary. We must simply say, "I will go and do the things which the Lord hath commanded" (1 Nephi 3:7).

We are to emulate Jesus, who "went about doing good,... for God was with him" (Acts 10:38). When we keep our hearts and minds attuned to His, we can be edified by the Spirit of the Lord and live in an inspired manner. "And if ye do always remember me ye shall have my Spirit to be with you" (3 Nephi 18:7).

Those who follow Jesus, do the things he has done, and always remember Him, will be privileged to rest with Him in the mansions of our Father. How blessed we will be to find pleasure in the face of God, as did Enos at the end of his mortal life. "And I soon go to the place of my rest, which is with my Redeemer; for I know that in him I shall rest. And I rejoice in the day when my mortal shall put on immortality, and shall stand before him; then shall I see his face with pleasure, and he will say unto me: Come unto me, ye blessed, there is a place prepared for you in the mansions of my Father. Amen" (Enos 1:27).

For additional insight see the following:

- B.H. Roberts, *The Gospel and Man's Relationship to Deity*, Salt Lake City, Deseret News, 1901.
- Bruce R. McConkie, "The Ten Blessings of the Priesthood," *Ensign*, Nov. 1977, 33–35.
- Glenn L. Pace, "Your Work Is Not Yet Finished," BYU Devotional, 11 Jan. 2005.
- Henry B. Eyring, "Always," CES Fireside, 3 Jan. 1999.
- Matthew, chapters 5 and 6.
- Mosiah, chapter 4, and 13:11–24.
- 3 Nephi, chapters 14 and 27.
- Alma, chapter 5.

Blessed are the pure in heart,
for they shall see God.
Matthew 5:8

Pure in Heart

Within the Book of Mormon, we read many sacred testimonials of prophets who saw and talked with Jesus Christ. While Moroni spent a great deal of time alone after the destruction of his people, he undoubtedly communed with the Lord often. As he bid farewell, his words were especially poignant:

> And now I, Moroni, bid farewell unto the Gentiles, yea, and also unto my brethren whom I love, until we shall meet before the judgment-seat of Christ....
> And then shall ye know that I have seen Jesus, and that he hath talked with me face to face,...
> "And now, I would commend you to seek this Jesus of whom the prophets and apostles have written. [Ether 12:38-39, 41]

Seek Jesus. Okay. Then I can be blessed to talk with Him face to face as did Moroni and other prophets? Perhaps it's not that simple. There is a qualifier: "Blessed are the pure in heart, for they shall see God" (Matthew 5:8). Pure in heart. I'm still working on that. Hence, my scriptural checklists in the previous chapter.

As a friend once said, "I used to be Snow White, but I drifted." There is hope in knowing our Savior atoned for our impurities. He continues to invite everyone, even the unrepentant, to come unto Him, as He asked the descendants of Lehi, "Will ye not now return unto me, and repent of your sins, and be converted, that I may heal you....

"If ye will come unto me ye shall have eternal life. Behold, mine arm of mercy is extended towards you, and whosoever will come, him will I receive; and blessed are those who come unto me (3 Nephi 9:13-14).

Those words were spoken after three days of destruction in the Promised Land. Imagine their devastated environment—ravaged by fire, upturned with earthquakes, swallowed in the sea, then engulfed in terrible, tangible darkness.

More than a decade ago, I authored a fictional book, *Through the Mists of Darkness*, set in those three catastrophic days in the Book of Mormon. During my research, I discovered many similarities between that period of time and the latter days. Before Jesus could visit the Nephite lands, there had to be a cleansing of the earth to humble the survivors and prepare them to meet Him. During the Last Days it's prophesied that great calamities and natural disasters will occur on the earth before the Lord's Second Coming.

Jesus Christ Will Come

Amid the many prophecies of the Advent of Christ, we are not provided an exact timetable of events. Rather, we are told, "Watch therefore, for ye know neither the day nor the hour wherein the Son of Man cometh" (Matthew 25:13). We will not be alerted in advance to roll out a red carpet, as is done for some VIPs. However, we do know Jesus will appear in red apparel to show He has "trodden the winepress alone" (Isaiah 63:3).

Following Christ's resurrection, "he was taken up; and a cloud received him" (Acts 1:9). Then two angels stood nearby and said, "This same Jesus, which is taken up from you into heaven, shall so come in like manner as ye have seen him go into heaven" (v. 11). We're not told if He went up in a whirlwind and chariot of fire like

Elijah (see 2 Kings 2:11). But it's not likely Jesus will return in a hot air balloon. However, this panorama view is prophesied:

> For as the light of the morning cometh out of the east, and shineth even unto the west, and covereth the whole earth, so shall also the coming of the Son of Man be....
> And then shall all the tribes of the earth mourn; and they shall see the Son of Man coming in the clouds of heaven, with power and great glory.
> And whoso treasureth up my word, shall not be deceived, for the Son of Man shall come, and he shall send his angels before him with the great sound of a trumpet, and they shall gather together the remainder of his elect from the four winds, from one end of heaven to the other. [JS-Matthew 1:26, 36-37]

I'm left to wonder in what state I shall be found—mourning with all the tribes, deceived because I have not treasured up God's word, or gathered among the elect. Because of the fragile nature of life on earth, it's possible I'll die before Christ's arrival. In that case, I hope I'm worthy to rise with "the saints that have slept" to meet Jesus "in the cloud" (D&C 45:45).

Our status will be better if we have fervently prayed for the millennial appearance of Jesus Christ. "Calling upon the name of the Lord day and night, saying: O that thou wouldst rend the heavens, that thou wouldst come down" (D&C 133:40). What a difference we might make if all Latter-day Saints would individually and collectively pray for the Second Coming!

Upon the Lord's triumphal entry to Jerusalem a week before He died, people laid down their clothing and palm branches along the way. They hailed Jesus with shouts of joy, saying:

> Blessed be the King that cometh in the name of the Lord: peace in heaven, and glory in the highest.
> And some of the Pharisees from among the multitude said unto him, Master, rebuke thy disciples.

And he answered and said unto them, I tell you that, if these should hold their peace, the stones would immediately cry out" (Luke 19:38-40).

Such convincing majesty in Jesus Christ that even the stones longed to proclaim His divinity! Then why are Latter-days Saints sometimes reluctant to testify of Him? Why are we afraid to open our mouths to proclaim the glorious events that soon will unfold? The answer might lie in our perceptions toward the Last Days and Second Coming. Most people respond in one of three ways:

- Ignorance or apathy from being too tangled in the cares of the world.
- Fear of destruction, or disbelief in its occurrence during our lifetime.
- Joyful anticipation and earnest prayers for His Kingdom to come.

How we could bless the world by rejoicing and sharing the glorious prospects of the Second Coming! The Last Days are upon us, and I believe the millennial reign of Jesus Christ is not far distant. As Elder Bruce R. McConkie wrote, "There will be an exact moment when his foot first touches the Mount of Olives.... And there will be a day and an hour and a split second that marks the beginning of the Millennium" (*The Millennial Messiah*, 649).

How I shall rejoice when "the glory of the Lord shall be revealed, and all flesh shall see it together" (Isaiah 40:5). What a thrill to be alive and hearken when "the Lord shall utter his voice, and all the ends of the earth shall hear it" (D&C 45:49). How amazing that the entire world will hear and see when "the Son of Man shall come in his glory, and all the holy angels with him" (Matthew 25:31). Even with so many miraculous manifestations, not all of God's children will understand nor believe what they witness. The Prophet Joseph Smith said, "Then will appear one grand sign of the Son of Man in heaven. But what will the world do? They will say it is a planet, a comet, etc. But the Son of Man

will come ... as the light of the morning cometh out of the east."
(*Teachings of the Prophet Joseph Smith,* 286 -287)

No matter each individual's view, all that has been prophesied
will be fulfilled. It's important to understand that "if ye are
prepared, ye shall not fear" (D&C 38:30).

> Wherefore, prepare ye, prepare ye, O my people; sanctify
> yourselves; gather ye together, O ye people of my church,...
> Prepare ye the way of the Lord, and make his paths straight,
> for the hour of his coming is nigh....
> And the Lord, even the Savior, shall stand in the midst of his
> people, and shall reign over all flesh (D&C 133:4, 17, 25).

Then comes the promise, "For since the beginning of the
world have not men heard nor perceived by the ear, neither hath
any eye seen, O God, besides thee, how great things thou hast
prepared for him that waiteth for thee" (D&C 133:45). Those who
do await, pray, and rejoice in the Lord's Second Coming, will have
exceptionally extraordinary experiences.

The Visitation of Jesus

My own desire to joyously await the Savior's Advent was
enhanced by authoring *Through the Mists of Darkness.* To compose
this fictional rendition of events in the Book of Mormon, I first had
to do research. Then I outlined the book by creating characters
who witnessed the three days of colossal darkness in the Western
Hemisphere after Jesus was crucified in Jerusalem. Originally, I
planned the book to include His visitation to the Promised Land.

While creating a novel, I try to see everything through
the viewpoint of the leading character. Then I write as if I'm
experiencing the story first-hand. In this case, the protagonist
was a sixteen-year-old young woman named Jael. Taken from a
woman's name in the Bible (see Judges, chapters 4 and 5), Jael is a
strong, symbolic name, since "Ja" stands for Jehovah and "el" for
Elohim. Looking at the world through the eyes of my fictional
Jael, I witnessed the tempests, earthquakes, and upheavals in the

Nephite lands. Then as darkness saturated her world, it was as if I felt the vile vapor seep into my own lungs, obstruct my sight, and shroud my body in gaseous blackness. Throughout the book, I endured three days of trials and triumphs with Jael in her unseen environment. As the darkness finally dissipated, I rejoiced with her family that their lives had been spared.

I then began to plot Christ's appearance in the land Bountiful, where Jael would travel with her mother. Yet when I attempted to write that glorious advent, I was unable to do it. My mere mortal words could not adequately portray that monumental scene. Nephi wrote, "no tongue can speak, neither can be written by any man, neither can the hearts of men conceive so great and marvelous things as we both saw and heard Jesus speak; and no one can conceive of the joy which filled our souls" (3 Nephi 17:17).

Though I failed to write about it, I was blessed to glimpse the sublime scene. It seemed I stood near the temple in the Land Bountiful as the wonders began. Through Jael, I sensed an aura of jubilant anticipation as the people conversed "about this Jesus Christ, of whom the sign had been given concerning his death" (3 Nephi 11:2).

At least 2500 people witnessed the Lord descending from heaven that day. Can you imagine the impact on each individual to personally see the Savior? Though I longed to describe the moment when they fell on their knees to worship Him, I could not do it. Nor could I express their feelings as they were invited to touch the tokens of His crucifixion and thrust their hands into His side where the sword had pierced His holy body.

I sensed their profound gratitude as He healed those with physical ailments who knelt at His feet. Yet I could not find words to adequately portray it. No matter my profound desire to share what I saw through the eyes of Jael, I was unable to include Christ's visitation in the final draft of my book.

Since then, I've yearned to be more ready and more worthy to witness the Second Coming of the Messiah. No matter if it occurs in the near or far future, I know that mortal words will never adequately express the joy of those who stand in His presence.

There is still much uncertainty concerning that blessed future day. But scriptures say our Father in Heaven will provide phenomenal signs and wonders to prepare His children to receive Jesus Christ. Though we sometimes dwell on the prophesied destruction, it's important to understand that many blessings will also be poured out upon the inhabitants of earth. Latter-day Saints can already see those miracles happening in everything from advanced technology to increased spiritual growth.

Global Missionary Work

More countries allow missionary work by the LDS Church than ever before. I didn't think I would see the Iron Curtain come down in my lifetime. But it happened. Missionaries now labor extensively throughout the former USSR and in other post-communist countries.

When my parents served in India during the 1980s they were only allowed to teach those who sought out the missionaries, which were few. Now there are a number of proselyting missionaries in India. My parents also went to Nigeria twice on missions, nine years apart. As they began their second round in 1989, they witnessed the first stake being created in that country. Membership in Nigeria continues to expand, and now the Aba Temple has opened its doors.

With China's improved economy and open policy to more Western influences, I believe the time for missionary work there is not far distant. I recently toured parts of China, including Tibet, where the Buddhist religion is prevalent. Humble yet happy, Tibetans seems particularly devout in their worship. I can see them quickly embracing the gospel once LDS missionaries are permitted to teach them.

In the summer of 2004, our oldest son moved his family to Hong Kong while he works in Shenzhen, China. Two of his sons are in elementary school, where the curriculum includes Mandarin Chinese. With that difficult language learned in their formative years, imagine how prepared those boys might be to someday serve missions in China.

The older of those two grandsons has already shown us he's not afraid to open his mouth. I'll never forget the day he stood with his two brothers alongside me and my husband on Main Street. We were in the median awaiting the arrival of Salt Lake's Trax commuter train. On the sidewalk opposite us, a man paced back and forth while shouting declarations of damnation to the wicked. Everyone near the self-proclaimed preacher looked askance, as if uneasy with the tirade. But only our six-year-old grandson had the courage to do anything. In the voice as loud as a boy can muster, our grandson called out to the man, "Why are you yelling? Why are you yelling?" Ten seconds later, the man walked quickly down the street and turned the corner out of our sight and hearing.

Missionary work will continue to be the prime means of adding converts to the Lord's fold, which exceeds twelve and a half million. The Church of Jesus Christ of Latter-day Saints is now the fourth largest in the United States (see "Church Fourth Largest in United States," *Ensign*, June 2005, 75). President Hinckley said, "The Church has grown across the world until our membership outside of North America exceeds that in North America. We have become a great international family scattered through 160 nations." ("Opening Remarks," *Ensign*, May 2005, 4-5)

In the same speech, our Prophet said "fifty-one million copies of the Book of Mormon [had] been distributed" during the ten years of his tenure. It is now available in 106 languages, and still counting. The Church recently entered into contract with Doubleday to publish and distribute copies of the Book of Mormon, in addition to those the Church prints and circulates. This widespread book recently appeared on a list of the 20 most profound books that have changed people's lives. (See "Book of Mormon one of the most influential," *Deseret Morning News*, 10 July 2003, A1)

Family History and Temple Work

During the last two decades of the twentieth century, there has been a family history explosion, and not just among Latter-day Saints. It has become a popular hobby for people worldwide to explore their family roots through genealogy.

As long as I can remember, my mother has been an avid and expert genealogist. I guess now I would have to call her an expert family historist. Family historian just doesn't sound right. Historist sounds more like naturalist, and that fits my mother, because family history seems to come naturally to her. Of course, those who do ancestral research know it never comes naturally— it is true work—an intense labor of love.

My own experience with family history has not been as productive as my mother's. I get easily discouraged when I can't find the names and dates I need, and I want to make up something to fill in the blanks. But it's not nice to feign the truth on something with eternal consequences. I've also thought of cheating on my four-generation family pedigree chart with oval photos of my ancestors. Some of their faces look so stern I've been tempted to use computer clip art to touch them up—cover a great-grandmother's face by adding a hat with a veil; replace a great-grandfather's frown with a nice shot of Clark Gable's smile. I suppose that would be fraud. Anyway, it shows my lack of confidence in family history work. Undoubtedly, I'll be a "skeleton in the closet" of my posterity.

I also will fail miserably if I'm asked how many temples have been erected in the world. I might stall for time by asking if they mean just LDS temples, or if I have to include all other religions with their temples. Eventually, I may stammer, "There are over a hundred and twenty LDS temples in operation." But at the rate the church is growing, I may never again be able to spout the correct response. It's best to rely on President Hinckley's knowledge:

> We have greatly increased the number of temples. In 1995, there were 47. Today, there are 119, with three more to be dedicated this year....
> We have constructed literally thousands of [ward and stake] buildings across the earth. They are of a better quality and more suitable to our needs than those previously built.

In addition, we have constructed this remarkable hall from which we speak today, the unique and beautiful Conference Center here in Salt Lake City. ["Opening Remarks," *Ensign*, May 2005, 5]

In March of 2000 before the Conference Center was open to the public, I had the privilege of touring the facility with other family members, because my brother Jon was one of the architects. We donned our hard hats and went to see the stunning auditorium with its padded seats still covered in protective plastic. Each of us took turns standing behind the yet-unstained, but famous, walnut wood pulpit. We pretended to be President Hinckley, from whose tree the pulpit was made. Jon then showed us where there was space to maneuver the rostrum into the background and make a stage for events other than conference. He took us far overhead in the catwalks where the lighting and other technical devices overlook the enormous auditorium. We also went behind the scenes to view the hefty trusses that suspend the balcony without the need of pillars. I felt the entire building was an inspired architectural idea from our Prophet Gordon B. Hinckley.

As we finished touring, we wondered if the Conference Center would be finished in three weeks to accommodate the April general conference. Jon said the Church would have to get a permit for temporary occupancy before the final inspection was completed. For some reason, I equated my vast tour of the Conference Center with visiting heaven. What if I'm allowed to enter the celestial kingdom for only temporary occupancy? How would I feel to glimpse that glory, but then have to leave it?

Technological Wonders

During April 2000 the first general conference was held in the new Conference Center. There Elder James E. Faust spoke about the advance of knowledge in the world:

I believe the future will be great and marvelous in many respects. Opportunities for education and learning have increased and will continue to increase dramatically. One person defined it this way: "Education is when you read the fine print. Experience is what you get if you don't" [Pete Seeger]. Now and in the future, vast amounts of information are becoming more accessible worldwide through electronic devices in the home, the workplace, or the local library....

I believe the appearance of God the Father and His Son, the Lord Jesus Christ, in 1820 to Joseph Smith unlocked the heavens not only to the great spiritual knowledge revealed in this dispensation but also to secular knowledge. ["The Shield of Faith," *Ensign*, May 2000, 18]

History proves that a vast array of inventions burst forth after the gospel was restored—everything from cotton gins to sewing machines, from electricity to nuclear power, from trains to automobiles, airplanes, jets, and rocketships. Domestic improvements increased dramatically from cranked telephones to cellular phones, from ringer washers to automatic washing machines—not to mention refrigerators, microwaves, air conditioners, and home theater systems.

Sometimes I feel breathless trying to keep up with technology's thundering development. In 1980 our family purchased a home computer that had two five-inch floppy disk drives and very little capacity—only 32K RAM. Now there are computers as small as the palm of your hand with a capability to contain whole libraries of information. How marvelous are these many advancements in knowledge, which are inspired by the heavens above, whether or not scientists and inventors believe it. Elder Harold B. Lee said, "No matter what his progress in science, man must always be subject to the will and direction of Divine Providence. Man has never discovered anything that God has not already known." ("Be Ye Not Deceived," BYU Speeches of the Year, 4 May 1965, 6)

Computer technology, telecommunications, transportation, satellite broadcasting, and countless other inventions are beneficial to the building of the kingdom of God on earth. "Through the miracle—and it is a miracle—of modern technology, these [conference] proceedings have been broadcast worldwide. Ninety-five percent of the membership of the Church in all the world could have participated with us." (Gordon B. Hinckley, "Closing Remarks," *Ensign*, May 2005, 102)

Granted, there are some negative side effects of improved technology, which may interrupt the flow of uplifting knowledge. An acronym used on the internet is WOMBAT, which stands for "waste of money, brains, and time." So much for thinking that wombats are Austrialian marsupials that can be snagged in a trap. Now wombats are snagging people!

Besides technological advancements in the world, the Church has improved the lives of countless people through the Perpetual Education Fund and LDS Humanitarian Aid. Also there is better comradery, rather than competition and hostility, between Latter-day Saints and many other religions.

Knowledge of medicine has improved humans' health so dramatically that countless lives are spared in cases that used to render quick death. It's also interesting that medical and scientific personnel have finally recognized the benefits of the Word of Wisdom (D&C 89) given by prophecy over 170 years ago.

All of these temporal and spiritual blessings, and others yet to be seen, are part of our Heavenly Father's plan to prepare His children for Christ's triumphal return to earth.

Signs and Prophecies

The Lord will not come unannounced. Several Old Testament prophecies preceded His birth. Nephites and Lamanites also foretold His nativity, mission, death, resurrection, and visit to the Promised Land. As the Second Coming nears, prophets and apostles will provide added revelation to guide the world. "We believe ... that [God] will yet reveal many great and important things pertaining to the Kingdom of God" (Articles of Faith 1:9).

In his book *Jesus the Christ*, Elder James E. Talmage wrote only one chapter, 14 pages, dealing with the Second Coming. At the start of that chapter, he stated: "The prophets of both hemispheres, who lived prior to the meridian of time, said comparatively little concerning the Lord's second coming" (p. 780).

Seven decades later, Elder Bruce R. McConkie wrote an entire book titled *The Millennial Messiah.*, published in 1982. Those 711 pages contain a wealth of information from ancient scripture in both hemispheres as well as modern-day revelation. It seems the heavens have already begun to disclose more about the last days. Remember, "he that believeth shall be blest with signs following, even as it is written.

"And unto you it shall be given to know the signs of the times, and the signs of the coming of the Son of man" (D&C 68:10-11).

Conclusion

My own patriarchal blessing provides a unique witness to me that the Lord's millennial reign is not far distant. In it is a reference to my children's purposes on earth. Not only are they to preach the word of God and prepare "this earth for the glorious second coming of the Lord," but also it states they will "witness the inauguration of His millennial reign as King of Kings and Lord of Lords, here upon this earth." [Patriarch Blessing given 3 December 1967]

Perhaps the line, "to witness the inauguration of His millennial reign" could mean that, whether alive or dead, they will witness that grand advent. But I like to take it literally—that at least one of my children will personally witness the Second Coming, which I believe is nearer than many of us like to think.

At that phenomenal apex in the history of earth, how thrilling to be worthy to behold our Savior's face! That blessing will be determined individually according to how we have lived our lives. Scriptures assure us that if we fill our souls with light and truth, we can be privileged to see the Lord:

And if your eye be single to my glory, your whole bodies shall be filled with light, and there shall be no darkness in you; and that body which is filled with light comprehendeth all things. Therefore, sanctify yourselves that your minds become single to God, and the days will come that you shall see him; for he will unveil his face unto you, and it shall be in his own time, and in his own way, and according to his own will. [D&C 88:67-68]

I want this promise to be mine as well as yours. How blessed our lives would be to witness what Joseph Smith and Sydney Rigdon saw in their vision of the three degrees of glory. They mightily testified so all of us would comprehend the reality of Jesus Christ.

And now, after the many testimonies which have been given of him, this is the testimony, last of all, which we give of him: That he lives!
For we saw him, even on the right hand of God; and we heard the voice bearing record that he is the Only Begotten of the Father. [D&C 76:22-23]

For additional insight see the following:

- Bruce R. McConkie, *The Promised Messiah*, Salt Lake City, Deseret Book Co., 1978, 570-615.
- Spencer V. Jones, "Finding Hope in the Second Coming," *Ensign*, June 2005, 38-40.
- Gordon B. Hinckley, "Opening Remarks," *Ensign*, May 2005, 5.
- Robert C. Oaks, "Who's on the Lord's Side? Who?" *Ensign*, May 2005, 48-50.

But we know that, when he shall appear,
we shall be like him; for we shall see him as he is.
1 John 3:2

When He Shall Appear

When will Jesus appear? How shall He arrive? Will you and I be there to witness His Second Coming? Will we "have confidence, and not be ashamed before him at his coming"? (1 John2:28) Might the earth be in such turmoil that only He can bring peace? How can we prepare, spiritually and temporally, for this climax of climaxes on the earth? Such questions might go on endlessly, because there is much we do not know. However, we must continue to look forward with hope in Christ, for "we know that, when he shall appear, we shall be like him; for we shall see him as he is.

"And every man that hath this hope in him purifieth himself, even as he is pure" (1 John 3:2-3).

No one can actually purify himself or herself without assistance from God. Sanctification occurs only by the power of Christ's Atonement through the Holy Spirit. That is the only way to become worthy and "like Him" at the time He shall appear unto us. Redemption is an individual journey, and not for the faint of heart. It's a demanding and fearsome mission for each child of God. No one else can repent and achieve exaltation in my place. No one can do it for you, except you.

One event that resembles what we know about Christ's Millennial Advent was His appearance at the temple in the Land Bountiful. How blessed were those who heard the Father proclaim, "Behold, my Beloved Son, in whom I am well pleased, in whom I have glorified my name" (see 3 Nephi 11:7).

What a rare blessing to hear the voice of God in their mortal ears! No wonder it took three times for them to understand His words, for "it did pierce them to the very soul, and did cause their hearts to burn" (v. 3). As the supernal message kindled both fear and rejoicing, they steadfastly looked upward and yearned to learn more. How awestruck they must have been when the Father asked them to regard His Son and "hear ye him" (v.7).

Although most mortals may not audibly hear the voice of God, our scriptures and latter-day prophets reveal His divine words. When we pay heed with all our might and minds, each sublime message can pierce our souls and cause our hearts to burn. All of us would undoubtedly fall on our knees in awe and worship if we saw the Lord and heard him say, "Behold, I am Jesus Christ, whom the prophets testified shall come into the world" (v.10).

Moses Saw God

Perhaps this is not a proper thing to say, but I've envied prophets like Moses, who "saw God face to face, and he talked with him, and the glory of God was upon Moses" (Moses 1:2). That entire first chapter of Moses is one I could read endlessly. After his personal encounter with God, Moses had a profound desire for all his people to have the same opportunity. Amid doctrine pertaining to the priesthood, several verses were written about Moses teaching the Israelites:

And this greater priesthood administereth the gospel and holdeth the key of the mysteries of the kingdom, even the key of the knowledge of God....

And without the ordinances thereof, and the authority of the priesthood, the power of godliness is not manifest unto men in the flesh;

For without this [Melchizedek priesthood] no man can see the face of God, even the Father, and live.

Now this Moses plainly taught to the children of Israel in the wilderness, and *sought diligently to sanctify his people that they might behold the face of God.*

But they hardened their hearts and could not endure his presence (D&C 84:19, 21-24, italics added).

Though Moses sought to sanctify his people so they might personally behold God, how sad that they hardened their hearts! I, too, have days when I am far too tangled in worldly ways to care about heavenly matters. Then I say to myself, "What do you think this is? Reality TV? Survivor? Who Wants to Be a Millionnaire? No! This life is part of your eternal life. Right now! This minute! So get busy and focus on things of eternal import!"

Daily, I must improve, as did those under the leadership of Nephi, the son of Helaman, who said, "Nevertheless they did fast and pray oft, and did wax stronger and stronger in their humility, and firmer and firmer in the faith of Christ, unto the filling their souls with joy and consolation, yea, even to the purifying and the sanctification of their hearts, which sanctification cometh because of their yielding their hearts unto God" (Helaman 3:35).

Joseph Smith Communed with God

It is through Joseph Smith that the heavens opened in these latter days so the glory of the Father and the Son could again be revealed to men on earth. How grateful I am for his youthful prayer in the sacred grove that resulted in the First Vision. This was not the only time Joseph testified of seeing the Lord. His vision with Oliver Cowdery, prior to the dedication of the Kirtland Temple was quite vivid.

We saw the Lord standing upon the breastwork of the pulpit, before us; and under his feet was a paved work of pure gold, in color like amber.

His eyes were as a flame of fire; the hair of his head was white
like the pure snow; his countenance shone above the brightness
of the sun; and his voice was as the sound of the rushing of
great waters, even the voice of Jehovah, saying:
I am the first and the last; I am he who liveth, I am he who was
slain; I am your advocate with the Father. [D&C 110:2-4].

What a hallowed privilege to see the Lord! I wonder if Joseph
and Oliver yearned to linger in His Presence. The feeling must
have permeated their hearts like fire. So unerasable were the
impressions within Oliver Cowdery that he offered this profound
counsel to the Twelve Apostles in his day:

It is necessary that you receive a testimony from heaven
for yourselves; so that you can bear testimony to the truth
of the Book of Mormon, and that you have seen the face of
God.... When you bear testimony that you have seen God,
this testimony God will never suffer to fall, but will bear you
out;...
Never cease striving until you have seen God face to face.
Strengthen your faith; cast off your doubts, your sins, and all
our unbelief; and nothing can prevent you from coming to God.
Your ordination is not full and complete till God has laid his
hand upon you. We require as much to qualify as did those who
have gone before us; God is the same. If the Savior in former
days laid his hands upon his disciples, why not in latter days?
[History of the Church, 2:195-196]

Latter-day Prophets and Apostles

To see the face of God is a sacred and hallowed blessing—one
that is rarely related in open dialogue to other people. Although
latter-day prophets and apostles may be privileged to see beyond
the veil, it's not often known by the general membership of the
church.

Through a granddaughter, President Lorenzo Snow shared
his face to face visit with Jesus Christ in the Salt Lake Temple.

Allie had been visiting her Grandpa Snow in his living quarters within the temple. On his way to let her out the front entrance, he paused in the corridor that led to the celestial room and said, "Wait a moment Allie, I want to tell you something. It was right here that the Lord Jesus Christ appeared to me at the time of the death of President Woodruff."

Allie saw her grandpa step nearer to her and hold out his left hand while saying, "He stood right here, about three feet above the floor. It looked as though He stood on a plate of solid gold." Then Allie related the following:

> Grandpa told me what a glorious personage the Savior is and described His hands, feet, countenance and beautiful, white robes, all of which were of such a glory of whiteness and brightness that he could hardly gaze upon Him.
>
> Then grandpa came another step nearer me and put his right hand on my head and said: "Now, granddaughter, I want you to remember that this is the testimony of your grandfather, that he told you with his own lips that he actually saw the Savior here in the Temple, and talked with Him face to face. [Allie Young Pond, *I Know That My Redeemer Lives: Latter-day Prophets Testify of the Savior*, 76-77.]

I revere anyone worthy of communing with the Lord face to face. Such a sacred event would probably leave the individual awestruck and weak, like Moses after he stood in the presence of God (see Moses 1:9-10). It seems logical that they would want to maintain the hallowed nature of their experiences, rather than chatting to everyone about it in casual conversations. That is all the more reason to hold dear the visions that are shared. The folloing is a testimony from Elder Orson F. Whitney a few years prior to his calling as one of the Twelve Apostles.

> I seemed to be in the Garden of Gethsemane, a witness of the Savior's agony. I saw Him as plainly as ever I have seen anyone.... The Son of God ... knelt and prayed. It was the

same prayer with which all Bible readers are familiar: "Oh my Father, if it be possible, let this cup pass from me; nevertheless not as I will, but as thou wilt."
As He prayed the tears streamed down his face, which was toward me. I was so moved at the sight that I also wept, out of pure sympathy. My whole heart went out to him; I loved him with all my soul, and longed to be with him as I longed for nothing else." [*Through Memory's Halls,* 82]

Perhaps you remember the conference address by Elder David B. Haight, who, in the midst of a health crisis, received a marvelous manifestation of the reality of Jesus Christ. Although Elder Haight recovered from this threat of death in 1989, he has since passed beyond this life into realms of glory. Yet his unique experience, shared in general conference, will always remain in our hearts.

After a serious operation, Elder Haight's life seemed to hang in the balance, so he pled with Heavenly Father to spare him a while longer. In the midst of his prayer, he lost consciousness. A siren from a paramedic truck was his last memory for several days. He said, "The terrible pain and commotion of people ceased. I was now in a calm, peaceful setting; all was serene and quiet...." Then he related the following:

I heard no voices but was conscious of being in a holy presence and atmosphere. During the hours and days that followed, there was impressed again and again upon my mind the eternal mission and exalted position of the Son of Man. I witness to you that He is Jesus the Christ, the Son of God, Savior to all, Redeemer of all mankind, Bestower of infinite love, mercy, and forgiveness, the Light and Life of the world. I knew this truth before—I had never doubted nor wondered. But now I knew, because of the impressions of the Spirit upon my heart and soul, these divine truths in a most unusual way.
I was shown a panoramic view of His earthly ministry: His baptism, His teaching, His healing the sick and lame, the mock trial, His crucifixion, His resurrection and ascension. There

followed scenes of His earthly ministry to my mind in impressive detail, confirming scriptural eyewitness accounts. I was being taught, and the eyes of my understanding were opened by the Holy Spirit of God so as to behold many things....

During those days of unconsciousness I was given, by the gift and power of the Holy Ghost, a more perfect knowledge of [Christ's] mission. I was also given a more complete understanding of what it means to exercise, in His name, the authority to unlock the mysteries of the kingdom of heaven for the salvation of all who are faithful. My soul was taught over and over again the events of the betrayal, the mock trial, the scourging of the flesh of even one of the Godhead. I witnessed His struggling up the hill in His weakened condition carrying the cross and His being stretched upon it as it lay on the ground, that the crude spikes could be driven with a mallet into His hands and wrists and feet to secure His body as it hung on the cross for public display.

Crucifixion—the horrible and painful death which He suffered—was chosen from the beginning. By that excruciating death, He descended below all things, as is recorded, that through His resurrection He would ascend above all things (See D&C 88:6).

I cannot begin to convey to you the deep impact that these scenes have confirmed upon my soul. ["The Sacrament—and the Sacrifice," *Ensign*, Nov. 1989, 59-60]

No doubt there are more apostolic accounts that could be told. However, I believe they are too sacred to share with the general public. For the time being, such uniquely-given memories are kept safely tucked in the hearts and minds of those who have received eyewitness testimonies of the Lord Jesus Christ.

The Veil Shall Be Rent

I believe that God is no respecter of persons and such divine experiences are available to the pure in heart—no matter their station or calling in life. My favorite scriptures are promises that ordinary Latter-day Saints can become worthy to see the face of God under certain conditions. You probably have your own favorite scriptures. But you'll have to write your own book in order to share them, or at least record them in your journal.

Ponder the following verse one phrase at a time: "Verily, thus saith the Lord: It shall come to pass that every soul who forsaketh his sins and cometh unto me, and calleth on my name, and obeyeth my voice, and keepeth my commandments, shall see my face and know that I am" (D&C 93:1-2).

Are any of those items too hard for mortal men and women to accomplish? Forsake our sins, come unto Christ, call on His name, obey Him, keep His commandments. We should desire to do everything within our power to become worthy to see the Redeemer of the world. "And again, verily I say unto you that is your privilege, and a promise I give unto you that ... inasmuch as you strip yourselves from jealousies and fears, and humble yourselves before me,... the veil shall be rent and you shall see me and know that I am" (D&C 67:10).

Though it's easy to apply these words to leaders of The Church of Jesus Christ of Latter-day Saints, these blessing are available to all worthy members. The Prophet Joseph Smith, who personally communed with the Savior on several occasions, verified that we could have revealed to us the things he knew. "This principle ought (in its proper place) to be taught, for God hath not revealed anything to Joseph, but what He will make known unto the Twelve, and even the least Saint may know all things as fast as he is able to bear them, for the day must come when no man need say to his neighbor, Know ye the Lord; for all shall know Him . . . from the least to the greatest" (*Teachings of the Prophet Joseph Smith*, 149).

Another verse from the Book of Mormon verifies this blessing. "And in that day that they shall exercise faith in me, saith the Lord, even as the brother of Jared did, that they may become sanctified in me, then will I manifest unto them the things which the brother of Jared saw, even to the unfolding unto them all my revelations, saith Jesus Christ, the Son of God, the Father of the heavens and of the earth, and all things that in them are" (Ether 4:7).

Certainly, it's a huge stretch to become as sanctified as the brother of Jared in order to see Jesus. But stretching the spirit is just as vital as stretching the physical body to keep it limber and active. Though I have no special calling in the leadership of the Church, I desire with all my heart to be worthy to personally witness the reality of Jesus Christ. You, too, can keep your mind and heart open to the possibility of this great miracle of revelation occurring in your life, as Elder Glenn L. Pace wrote:

There are blessings available to those who have become substantially purified or sanctified, blessings that are reserved for the pure in heart....

Since God is no respecter of persons, all who purify and sanctify their lives ... have access to learning the mysteries of the kingdom....

It should go without saying that the blessings are available to male and female alike. We sometimes confuse the privilege of holding the priesthood with the blessings of the priesthood....

I reemphasize that God is no respecter of persons, and that these blessings come as a result of purity, not position....

It comes after a trial of faith. [*Spiritual Plateaus*, 117, 127-128, 134]

Few people look forward to trials of faith. But few can escape adversity in this unpredictable world. It's heartening to know that blessings on earth and eternal rewards are offered to those who, in the midst of hardships, steadfastly remain true to their faith in Jesus Christ.

We Shall See the Face of God

When I was the typical hassled mother with four young children, it was difficult—if not impossible—to listen with full concentration to general conference. However, it would have been more of a strain to hear King Benjamin when he spoke to families who had pitched their tents toward the high tower where he stood.

Because that crowd was vast in number, King Benjamin had his words written and circulated to those not within the sound of his voice. Likewise, Latter-day Saints are blessed to have conference addresses written and circulated in our church magazines. Perhaps you read and underline your May and November editions of the *Ensign* or *Liahona* as if they were scriptures. If not, it's never too late to begin. Remember, you can only be late when you're in view of a clock. And with God, there is no timekeeping. It's never too late to indulge yourself in a thorough study of His words—whether from ancient scripture or latter-day prophets and apostles.

I'm grateful for the meaningful messages we receive from those called and ordained as special witnesses to Jesus Christ. Toward the end of his mortal life, Elder Bruce R. McConkie shared this unwavering testimony of the Savior:

And now, as pertaining to this perfect atonement, wrought by the shedding of the blood of God—I testify that it took place in Gethsemane and at Golgotha, and as pertaining to Jesus Christ, I testify that he is the Son of the Living God and was crucified for the sins of the world. He is our Lord, our God, and our King. This I know of myself independent of any other person.

I am one of his witnesses, and in a coming day I shall feel the nail marks in his hands and in his feet and shall wet his feet with my tears.

But I shall not know any better then than I know now that he is God's Almighty Son, that he is our Savior and Redeemer, and that salvation comes in and through his atoning blood and in no other way. ["The Purifying Power of Gethsemane," *Ensign*, May 1985, 11]

Those words imply that the Lord Jesus Christ personally revealed himself to Elder McConkie. In the same manner Moses sought to sanctify his people that they might see God, Elder McConkie provided this edifying message to righteous individuals:

As believing saints it is our privilege:

1. To enjoy the gift of the Holy Ghost; to receive personal revelation; to possess the signs that always follow true believers, to work miracles; and to have the gifts of the Spirit, and

2. To see the Lord face to face; to talk with him as a man speaketh with his friend; to have his Person attend us from time to time; and to have him manifest to us the Father....

After they make their calling and election sure and prove themselves worthy of every trust . . . it becomes their right and privilege to see the Lord and commune with him face to face. Revelations, visions, angelic visitations, the rending of the heavens, and appearances among men of the Lord himself—all these things are for all of the faithful. They are not reserved for apostles and prophets only. God is no respecter of persons. They are not reserved for one age only, or for a select lineage of people. We are all our Father's children (*The Promised Messiah*, 571, 575).

With all the intensity of my heart I believe I can live in such a way to someday behold our Savior's face. And so can you! Whether that occurs in this mortal life, or in the eternal realms ahead, all will be done according the wisdom of God for each individual. What joy will permeate our souls on that humbling occasion! "And it shall be said in that day, Lo, this is our God; we have waited for him, and he will save us: this is the Lord; we have waited for him, we will be glad and rejoice in his salvation" (Isaiah 25:9).

We don't have to wait to be glad and rejoice in the salvation Christ offers. Perhaps we can purify our lives to the extent that we can behold Him while yet in the flesh (see D&C 76:116-118). Or perhaps we will be privileged to see the Lord return in glory to reign on earth. Elder Bruce R. McConkie proclaimed, "We have the power—and it is our privilege—so to live, that becoming pure in heart, we shall see the face of God while we yet dwell as mortals in a world of sin and sorrow." ("The Ten Blessings of the Priesthood, *Ensign*, Nov. 1977, 34)

Most days I feel terribly unqualified to ever be in Christ's presence. When, and if, I arrive at the gates of heaven, I hope I don't have to stand trial for destruction of God-issued equipment— meaning my divine spirit. Rather, I hope to be worthy of all God's blessings and to be a joint heir with Christ in our Father's kingdom (see Romans 8:17).

I wonder how my attitudes and actions would change at this point in my life with one glimpse of Christ's face. How would I feel to have His eyes penetrate my soul, His warm smile shine upon me, and His voice speak my name? Though it's doubtful I will actually see Jesus with my mortal eyes, there is nothing to prevent me from living as if I've already had that privilege.

Conclusion

How blessed we are to prayerfully and joyfully anticipate the return of Jesus Christ, when all the world "shall see the Son of man coming in clouds of heaven with power and great glory" (Matthew 24:30). Don't worry, Relief Society sisters won't be asked to bring refreshments to this grand occasion. Nor will it matter how we dress, though modesty is a virtue. Jesus will be washing our unclean garments anyway. If worthy, we will be given new white robes and crowns of glory.

What a wondrous time it shall be as His millennial reign begins! Can you step back from your mortality for a moment and glimpse the splendor and majesty of the Lord's coming, as John Taylor stated, "The Lord will be king over all the earth, and all mankind literally under his sovereignty, and every nation under the heavens will have to acknowledge his authority, and bow to his sceptre. Those who serve him in righteousness will have communication with God, and with Jesus; will have the ministering of angels, and will know the past, the present, and the future." (*The Government of God*, Liverpool, S. W. Richards, 97)

It may be far beyond our human view to imagine communing with God the Father and Jesus Christ during the Millennium. How will we act while knowing the past, present, and future of our lives all at once (see D&C 130:6-9)? Will we be worthy to witness the heralding trumpets, rejoicing angels, and bright glory ushering Christ to earth? What possible callings might you and I receive to bring to pass righteousness in this colossal Kingdom of God? These and other questions will ultimately be answered by our degree of devotion to the Lord. "For the Son of man shall come in the glory of his Father with his angels; and then he shall reward every man according to his works" (Matthew 16:27).

Wherever we stand at that day—righteous, wicked, or simply indifferent—the eternal plan of God will go forth. All His words will be fulfilled, as Joseph Smith proclaimed:

> The standard of Truth has been erected. No unhallowed hand can stop the work from progressing; persecutions may rage, mobs may combine, armies may assemble, calumny may defame, but the truth of God will go forth boldly, nobly, and independent, till it has penetrated every continent, visited every clime, swept every country, and sounded in every ear, till the purposes of God shall be accomplished, and the Great Jehovah shall say the work is done. (*History of the Church*, 4:540).

How blessed will be the righteous, who unceasingly labor in preparing the world to herald the King of kings! This indeed is "a marvelous work and a wonder" (Isaiah 29:14).

May we be glad and rejoice in Jesus Christ every moment of our lives, that "when he shall appear, we shall be like him; for we shall see him as he is" (1 John 3:2).

For additional insight see the following:

- Gerald N. Lund, *The Coming of the Lord*, Salt Lake City, Bookcraft, 1971.
- James E. Talmage, *Jesus the Christ*, Deseret Book Co., Salt Lake City, first printing 1915.
- Bruce R. McConkie, *The Millennial Messiah*, Deseret Book Co., Salt Lake City, 1982.
- M. Russell Ballard, "The Joy of Hope Fulfilled," *Ensign*, November 1992, 30-32.
- Glenn L. Pace, *Spiritual Plateaus*, Salt Lake City, Deseret Book Co., 1991.

Appendix
Bibliography

Benson, Ezra Taft. *The Teachings of Ezra Taft Benson*. Salt Lake City, Bookcraft, 1988.

Children's Songbook. Salt Lake City. The Church of Jesus Christ of Latter-day Saints, 1989.

Collected Discourses. Edited by Brian H. Stuy. 5 vols. Sandy, BHS Publishing, 1992.

Devotional Speeches of the Year. Provo, BYU Publications, 1977.

Holy Bible, Authorized King James Version. Salt Lake City, The Church of Jesus Christ of Latter-day Saints, 1979.

Hymns of The Church of Jesus Christ of Latter-day Saints. Salt Lake City, The Church of Jesus Christ of Latter-day Saints, 1985.

I Know That My Redeemer Lives: Latter-day Prophets Testify of the Savior. Salt Lake City, Deseret Book, 1990.

Kimball, Spencer W. *Hidden Wedges*. Salt Lake City, Deseret Book, 1974.

Kimball, Spencer W. *Faith Precedes the Miracle*. Salt Lake City, Deseret Book, 1972.

Kimball, Spencer W. *The Miracle of Forgiveness*. Salt Lake City, Bookcraft, 1969.

Lewis, C. S. *Mere Christianity.* MacMillian Publishing Co., New York, 1952.

Madsen, Truman G. *Eternal Man.* Salt Lake City, Deseret Book, 1966.

Maxwell, Neal A. *The Neal A. Maxwell Quote Book.* Salt Lake City, Bookcraft, 1997.

McConkie, Bruce R. *The Millennial Messiah: The First Coming of Christ.* Salt Lake City, Deseret Book, 1978.

McConkie, Bruce R. *The Promised Messiah: The Second Coming of the Son of Man.* Salt Lake City, Deseret Book, 1982.

Mother Teresa. *No Greater Love.* Novato, New World Library, 1997.

Robinson, Bonnie B. *Through the Mists of Darkness,* American Fork, Covenant Communications, Inc., 1994.

Smith, Joseph. *History of the Church.* Salt Lake City, Deseret Book, 1978.

Smith, Joseph. *Lectures on Faith.* Salt Lake City, Deseret Book, 1985.

Smith, Joseph, translator. *The Book of Mormon.* Salt Lake City, The Church of Jesus Christ of Latter-day Saints, 1981.

Smith, Joseph. *The Doctrine and Covenants.* Salt Lake City, The Church of Jesus Christ of Latter-day Saints, 1981.

Smith, Joseph. *The Pearl of Great Price.* Salt Lake City, The Church of Jesus Christ of Latter-day Saints, 1981.

Smith, Joseph. *Teachings of the Prophet Joseph Smith.* Salt Lake City, Deseret Book, 1976.

Talmage, James E. *Jesus the Christ.* Salt Lake City, Deseret Book, 1973.

Webster's Third New International Dictionary of the English Language, unabridged. Philip Babcock Gove, Editor. Springfield, Merriam-Webster Inc., 1961; reprint 1986.

Young, Brigham. *Discourses of Brigham Young, vol. 9 & 10* arranged by John A. Widtsoe. Salt Lake City, Deseret Book, 1954.

Index

After reading *When He Shall Appear* you'll want to read the companion book *We Shall Be Like Him*, due to be published during late autumn of 2006. To get updates on its progress, check with www.bonfirepress.com or with your favorite bookstore where LDS products are sold.

Bonfire Press, LC

We Shall Be Like Him

Bonnie B. Robinson

The following pages are a sneak preview
into the book *We Shall Be Like Him.*

Read this prologue to prepare for the book's
coming out party. But don't drool over the
content of it. You'll get the pages all wet.

When he shall appear,
we shall be like him;
for we shall see him as he is.
Moroni 7:48
Book of Mormon

Prologue
We Shall Be Like Him

At first it seemed surreal, as if I were inside a three dimensional movie. Yet right before my eyes was the sign for the Garden Tomb, outside the walled city of Jerusalem. With a BYU tour to the Holy Land, I had been appointed as "tribe scribe" to chronicle our two-week trip and distribute the record to our group. While scribbling sentences in my notebook, I followed our guide toward a bench-lined gazebo, where lavender bougainvillea draped the roof. (Until then, bougainvillea was not part of my vocabulary, and even now my computer spell checker is in shock with such a dramatic word.) I enjoyed how the blossoms' mellow aroma mingled with other earthy scents in the spring-green garden.

Within the gazebo, I settled onto a wooden bench amid our tour group. My heart hiccupped when I saw not far away the hill called Calvary. *Incredible!* I thought. *I am actually here where Jesus died. This is reality—not a TV documentary. Time for a spirituality upgrade. Forget about world peace. Just aim for peace in your own heart.*

Though a pang of sorrow creased my soul, I continued to stare at the oft-photographed outcropping of rocks that resembled a skull. Calvary. Golgotha. Much more than mere names. A hallowed yet fearful place where Jesus was nailed on a cross of wood, and where eternal life and salvation hung in the balance. *Time for me to surrender,* I decided. *Time to stop pretending I'm something better than I am. I'll put up the white flag. Jesus has won my soul once again. He is always victorious. Truly He has overcome all things, including my stubborn human nature.*

Atop the hill stood telephone poles, which vividly conveyed a symbolic cross on which our Savior was crucified. After being in the Holy Land for six days, I felt anchored with a tangible grasp of Christ's life on earth. But nothing I'd seen could compare to this scene depicting His death, anguish, sacrifice, suffering, and Atonement. A lump of sorrow choked in my throat.

Our guide began to relate the account of Christ's final hours on earth. Beneath the ebb and flow of his words, my self-examination mushroomed. *Why had I sat down? I should be on my feet pacing. Or better yet, on my knees repenting.* I stood up, offered my seat to another woman, then leaned against a pillar on a shadowed edge of the gazebo, where I could conceal the tears that wedged through my eyelids.

Behind me, I heard soft singing from another group in the garden. Though I didn't understand their foreign words, the music reverenced this holy place.

I could no longer see Calvary, yet some members of our group still gazed upon the fateful hillside. Despite the suffusive tranquility of the garden and the soft-spoken words of our guide, no one dozed off, as had occurred earlier in the week due to jet lag. I knew today's red-rimmed eyes were not from fatigue but from humble gratitude for the Savior. Several people wiped moisture from their cheeks.

Our guide gestured to the far corner of the garden where we would soon view the treasured tomb. *So close! Why am I just standing here? My feet aren't super-glued to the stone pavement.* An unseen force began to tug on me. Still endeavoring to jot down the words of our guide, I edged away from the gazebo. Then I tiptoed past the singing foreigners, whose hymn faded with a series of "amens." I felt cocooned in silence and solace, which eased the tears that had clouded my view. Now I could more easily follow the short path toward the hallowed sepulcher. Above me, it seemed the rustling leaves whispered that the Spirit of the Lord was near.

My footsteps halted on tree-shadowed overlook. I glanced down at the stone-carved sepulcher. My breathing ceased. I could no longer take notes. I dared not move nor do anything to disturb the profound moment. A sudden surge of spiritual power thrust through my heart and made it pound like a tom-tom. I folded my arms and pressed my notebook against my chest to contain the throbbing. The Spirit bore a vivid witness: *Jesus had been crucified and was laid in this tomb. Yet He truly did arise on the third day.*

My eyes could not unfasten their gaze on the rectangular hole that had once been covered by a rolling stone. *This sacred site is where Jesus Christ was resurrected. He has been in this garden!* I used one hand to cover my lips that wanted to shout for joy. My thumping heart increased its speed. Uncanny thoughts jammed in my mind: *Jesus was here long ago, and He is here again! Right now! Right behind you! Just turn around!*

I took in a trembling breath. *Do I dare look? Am I prepared to be in Christ's presence? Is there is a dress code? A behavior code? Should I smile and look into His face or fall at His feet in worship?* With both anxiety and reverence, I slowly rotated my head to glance over my shoulder. Certain He was close, I blinked several times in an effort to see Him. But I could discern no Holy Being. Only trees and flowers and stones amid the peaceful garden.

Although I saw nothing unusual, I felt a flood of love drench my soul. And then, as faint as a snowflake striking a windowpane, I heard a sound. *Was it my name? Did a hushed voice speak my name, just as Mary Magdalene had heard her own name near this Garden Tomb?* I wasn't certain. Yet how I wished it were true! Even as I write this, I still yearn for the day when the Savior calls me by name and beckons for me to come near.

Never did I want that moment of pure love to end! But alas, the Garden Tomb is a public place, and within a few minutes I found myself swept back in the midst of our tour group. I followed them down a set of stairs to get a closer look at the tomb. While awaiting my turn to enter, I pondered the story of when "[Mary] saw Jesus standing and knew not that it was Jesus" (John 20:14). Then I wondered, *Will I know Jesus well enough to recognize Him when I see Him?*

"Jesus saith unto her, Woman, why weepest thou? whom seekest thou?" (John 20:15). Then I had to ask myself, *Am I earnestly seeking Jesus in my day-to-day life? How can I qualify to stand in His presence? Do I truly exhibit an insatiable quest to become like Him?*

"If you really want to *be* like the Lord—more than any *thing* or *anyone* else—you must remember that your adoration of Jesus is best shown by your emulation of Him." (Russell M. Nelson, "Endure and Be Lifted Up," *Ensign,* May 1997, 72, italics in the original)

Never before and never after that soul-filling day at the Garden Tomb have I experienced such a profound encounter with the Divine. How I long to once again feel that indescribable love—the pure love of Christ! And how I wish I could share it with others!

Amid these pages and the companion book *When He Shall Appear,* I will offer ideas gleaned in my embarking on that pathway of pure love. I invite you to walk with me in this heart-energizing quest to become like Him.

"Wherefore,... pray unto the Father with all the energy of heart, that ye may be filled with this love,... that when he shall appear **we shall be like him**" (Moroni 7:48).

About the Author

One of Bonnie Bradshaw Robinson's goals is to meet every person in the world. That either demonstrates she's quite fond of people or she's a little off her rocker. Truth is, she rarely has time to sit in her rocker. Busy traveling to various locations around the globe with her husband, Glenn, and visiting their four childrens' families, Bonnie also likes to camp, hike, snowshoe, ski, sing, play guitar and dulcimer, go to the temple, chat with friends, and—well, you get the picture. Bonnie is especially thrilled if she can sit down to read a book. Most of her reading is done while walking for exercise in the canyon near her Salt Lake City home.

A woman of "exceedingly great faith" (Moroni 10:11), Bonnie is somewhat of a risktaker, living life with joyful anticipation of new adventures. Should you wish her to venture into your part of the world for speaking at a fireside or youth conference, please contact her through bonfirepress.com.